YORK NOTES

C000257019

# THE TAMING OF THE SHREW

## WILLIAM SHAKESPEARE

**Notes by Rebecca Warren**
**Revised by Frances Gray**

PEARSON

YORK PRESS

YORK PRESS
322 Old Brompton Road, London SW5 9JH

PEARSON EDUCATION LIMITED
Edinburgh Gate, Harlow,
Essex CM20 2JE, United Kingdom
Associated companies, branches and representatives throughout the world

First published 1999
New edition 2005
This new and fully revised edition 2015

10 9 8 7 6 5 4 3

ISBN 978-1-4479-8227-2

Illustration on p. 41 by Alan Batley
Phototypeset by Border Consultants
Printed in Slovakia

Photo credits: Lance Bellers/Shutterstock for page 7 middle / DarkBird/Shutterstock for page 8 middle / Erni/Shutterstock for page 9 bottom / Birgit Reitz-Hofmann/Shutterstock for page 10 bottom / val lawless/Shutterstock for page 12 middle / cynoclub/Shutterstock for page 13 top / Kiselev Andrey Valrevich/Shutterstock for page 13 bottom / showcake/Shutterstock for page 15 bottom / DarkBird/Shutterstock for page 16 middle / Nick_Nick/Shutterstock for page 17 bottom / photo.ua/Shutterstock for page 19 top / Ugorenkov Aleksandr/Shutterstock for page 20 top / Graham Taylor/Shutterstock for page 21 top / Marcin Niemiec/Shutterstock for page 22 middle / cenap_refik ongan/Shutterstock for page 23 top / Kanea/Shutterstock for page 25 bottom / Isantilli/Shutterstock for page 26 bottom / Bronwyn Photo/Shutterstock for page 27 bottom / Unholy Vault Designs/Shutterstock for page 28 top / Chris Hill/Shutterstock for page 29 top / silky/Shutterstock for page 30 middle / tanewpix/Shutterstock for page 32 top / Computer Earth/Shutterstock for page 33 top / Mega Pixel/Shutterstock for page 34 top / Ocskay Bence/Shutterstock for page 34 bottom / © itanistock/Alamy for page 35 top / Nordling/Shutterstock for page 36 middle / Paul Matthew Photography/Shutterstock for page 37 bottom / skydie/Shutterstock for page 38 bottom / Olena Teslya/Shutterstock for page 40 bottom / Distrikt 3/Shutterstock for page 42 top / Distrikt 3/Shutterstock for page 43 middle / DarkBird/Shutterstock for page 44 top / Ian Schofield/Shutterstock for page 45 top / ©itanistock/Alamy for page 46 top / Carpeira/Shutterstock for page 46 bottom / David Lyons/Alamy for page 47 top / Radu Razvan/Shutterstock for page 48 top / BortN66/Shutterstock for page 49 top / Surkov Dimitri/Shutterstock for page 50 middle / LUCARELLI TEMISTOCLE/Shutterstock for page 51 middle / Kachalkina Veronika/Shutterstock for page 52 top / rangizzz/Shutterstock for page 54 top / artcasta/Shutterstock for page 55 bottom / AlbleStock.com/Thinkstock for page 57 top / Aleksei Gurko/Shutterstock for page 58 middle / Korolevskaya Nataliya/Shutterstock for page 60 bottom / PHOTOCREO Michal Bednarek/Shutterstock for page 62 bottom / HLPhoto/Shutterstock for page 64 bottom / BEPictured/Shutterstock for page 65 top / St. Nick/Shutterstock for page 65 middle / Tom Reichner/Shutterstock for page 66 bottom / acceptphoto/Shutterstock for page 67 top / Corbis images/Halfdark for page 68 bottom / © iStock/TonyBagget for page 71 bottom / Florin Stana/Shutterstock for page 72 top / s74/Shutterstock for page 73 middle / wavebreakmedia/Shutterstock for page 74 bottom / Portrait Essentials/Alamy for page 75 top / optimarc/Shutterstock for page 75 bottom / Amawasri Pakdara/Shutterstock for page 76 bottom / © iStock/nullplus for page 77 top

# CONTENTS

# PART FIVE: CONTEXTS AND INTERPRETATIONS

# PART SIX: PROGRESS BOOSTER

# PART SEVEN: FURTHER STUDY AND ANSWERS

# HOW TO STUDY *THE TAMING OF THE SHREW*

These York Notes can be used in a range of ways to help you read, study and revise for your exam or assessment.

## Become an informed and independent reader

Throughout the Notes, you will find the following key features to aid your study:

- **Key context** margin features: these will help to widen your knowledge of the setting, whether historical, social or political. They are highlighted by the AO3 (Assessment Objective 3) symbol to remind you of the connection to aspects you may want to refer to in your exam responses.

- **Key interpretation** boxes (a key part of AO5): do you agree with the perspective or idea that is explained here? Does it help you form your own view on events or characters? Developing your own interpretations is a key element of higher level achievement at A Level, so make use of this and similar features.

- **Key connection** features (linked to AO4): whether or not you refer to such connections in your exam writing, having a wider understanding of how the play, or aspects of it, links to other texts or ideas, can give you new perspectives on the text.

- **Study focus** panels: these will help you to secure your own understanding of key elements of the text. Being able to write in depth on a particular point, or explain a specific feature, will help your writing sound professional and informed.

- **Key quotation** features: these identify the effect of specific language choices – you could use these for revision purposes at a later date.

- **Progress booster** features: these offer specific advice about how to tackle a particular aspect of your study, or an idea you might want to consider discussing in your exam responses.

- **Extract analysis** sections: these are vital for you to use either during your reading, or when you come back to the text afterwards. These sections take a core extract from a scene and explore it in real depth, explaining its significance and impact, raising questions, and offering interpretations.

## Stay on track with your study and revision

Your first port of call will always be your teacher, and you should already have a good sense of how well you are doing, but the Notes offer you several ways of measuring your progress.

- **Revision task**: throughout the Notes, there are some challenging, but achievable, written tasks for you to do relevant to the section just covered. Suggested answers are supplied in **Part Seven**.

- **Progress check**: this feature comes at the end of **Parts Two** to **Five**, and contains a range of short and longer tasks which address key aspects of the Part of the Notes you have just read. Below this is a grid of key skills which you can complete to track your progress, and rate your understanding.

- **Practice task** and **Mark scheme**: use these features to make a judgement on how well you know the text and how well you can apply the skills you have learned.

**The text used in these Notes is the Arden Shakespeare, 2010.**

---

**A02** PROGRESS BOOSTER

You can choose to use the Notes as you wish, but as you read the play, it can be useful to read over the **Part Two** summaries and analysis in order to embed key events, ideas and developments in the narrative.

---

**A02** PROGRESS BOOSTER

Don't forget to make full use of Parts Three to Five of the Notes during your reading of the play. You may have essays to complete on genre, or key themes, or on the impact of specific settings, and can therefore make use of these in-depth sections. Or you may simply want to check out a particular idea or area as you're reading or studying the play in class.

---

**A01** PROGRESS BOOSTER

**Part Six: Progress Booster** will introduce you to different styles of question and how to tackle them; help you to improve your expression so that it has a suitably academic and professional tone; assist you with planning and the use of evidence to support ideas, and, most importantly, show you three sample exam responses at different levels with helpful AO-related annotations and follow-up comments. Dedicating time to working through this Part will be time you won't regret.

# THE TAMING OF THE SHREW: A SNAPSHOT

## Join the debate

In *The Taming of the Shrew*, a rich man forces his oldest – and troublesome – daughter to get married. Her husband employs a variety of methods to curb his bride's headstrong attitude: he deprives her of food, sleep and new clothes, and bombards her with lectures about obedience, until she finally acts in a way that pleases him. The story might be summarised crudely as 'a bad-tempered woman learns to behave', or as 'the heroine is forced to submit to a bully'. Audiences have debated both points of view for four centuries.

## Happily ever after?

*The Taming of the Shrew* presents itself as a **comedy**; there are many definitions of this word, but all of them involve the idea of a happy ending. Modern audiences rarely find Shakespeare's ending straightforwardly 'happy' and have even been known to boo or to picket the theatre. Yet *The Taming of the Shrew* remains stubbornly popular and rarely fails to do well at the box office.

## Varieties of comedy

One reason for the play's popularity is its exuberant mix of comic styles. Petruccio, the tamer, is energetic, confident and funny; Katherina, the 'shrew', matches his wit and fire. Their scenes are packed with clever cross-talk and sometimes slapstick comedy. They contrast with the characters of the subplot, a slick, more conventional Italian romantic comedy centred on Katherina's sister Bianca, who marries the man she wants via trickery and disguise.

Both plots comprise a play-within-a-play which is framed by the **Induction**. The Induction shows how a nobleman and a band of players stage a play (*The Taming of the Shrew*) to entertain a drunk, Christopher Sly, who has been thrown out of a tavern after a roaring argument with its female owner. The role of Sly offers opportunities for an extrovert actor to play a larger-than-life, but recognisable, character. The Induction, however, is also a reminder that the shrew-taming is 'only a story', prompting us to think for ourselves about the kind of story presented to Sly – and, perhaps, to compare our reactions to his.

## Men and women

Under Elizabeth I, the English Protestant Church stressed the virtues of marriage and family, prompting debate about the position of women. Marriage was not considered an equal partnership – Katherina's speech in Act V about wifely obedience embodies the orthodox view – but some degree of female consent was important. Love and fidelity could not be expected from a domestic slave. The stage became one laboratory for exploring gender relationships. Shakespeare examines forced marriage and free choice in both comic and serious plays. *The Taming of the Shrew,* however, is his only comedy showing a woman forced to marry and being punished for speaking her mind.

This may always have troubled some spectators. Most adaptations of *The Taming of the Shrew*, from Fletcher's play *The Tamer Tamed* (1611) to the teen movie *10 Things I Hate About You* (1999), set up their plots so that the heroine is not trapped from the outset. In Shakespeare's own later comedy *Much Ado About Nothing* (*c*.1598) the heroine Beatrice mocks men and marries on her terms.

**KEY INTERPRETATION**  **A05**

You can read about reactions to some modern productions of *The Taming of the Shrew*, and a discussion of how actors and directors have set about dealing with some of the problems it presents, in Michael Mangan's *A Preface to Shakespeare's Comedies 1594–1603* (1996).

**KEY INTERPRETATION** **A05**

In 1897 the playwright George Bernard Shaw, a keen advocate of women's rights, described the play as 'altogether disgusting to modern sentiments' and suggested it should no longer be staged. Is there a case for banning *The Taming of the Shrew*?

# A new playwright for a new theatre

When Shakespeare arrived in London as a young man in his twenties, the theatre was a bold career choice. The first professional companies performing full-length dramas were formed when he was a boy. The oldest theatre building – called simply The Theatre – was only about ten years old; new ones such as the Swan and the Curtain were springing up, packing in audiences of around two thousand with a different play every day. Actors and writers were only beginning to explore the possibilities of this exciting new medium. The open stage, with no scene changes, let the action move fast and encouraged vividly contrasting scenes. The open-air, daylight performances created a lively relationship between actor and audience – if there was a risk of heckling, there were also chances for the actor to speak very directly to his audience.

Shakespeare experimented with characters who are also spectators, like Sly in the Induction. By 1592 he had a growing reputation as an actor and playwright. By 1594 he was working

with a single company, the Lord Chamberlain's Men, drawing on their particular talents. Besides one tragedy and several plays of English history he had explored varieties of comedy – farce in *The Comedy of Errors*, romantic Italian comedy in *The Two Gentlemen of Verona* – and had probably also written *The Taming of the Shrew*.

## The text

Shakespeare's plays were not published in his lifetime. Scripts were a valuable resource and companies did not want them to be available to other actors. A play text called *The Taming of A Shrew* did appear in 1594, but it is not clear whether this was an earlier version written by Shakespeare or an attempt by a rival company to create a 'pirate' text. However, there is no final, definitive version of *The Taming of the Shrew*. Shakespeare wrote for a working company. He might add material contributed in rehearsal by the actors, delete jokes that did not get laughs, add topical allusions or remove characters to suit a smaller cast when the company went on tour. The Arden edition on which this book is based outlines important differences in various early editions of the play, but Shakespeare probably viewed all his plays as 'work in progress'.

**A02**

## Study focus: Key issues to explore

As you study the text and revise for the exam, keep in mind these key elements:
- Creating comedy – romance, slapstick, wordplay
- Ideas of love and marriage
- Power relationships – between man and woman, master and servant
- Games, disguises and role-playing
- Parents and children
- How text and performer interact to interpret a character

# SYNOPSIS

## Induction: Watching the play

A drunken tinker, Christopher Sly, staggers out of a Warwickshire tavern, the angry Hostess threatening him with arrest. He falls asleep and is found by a hunting party. The Lord in command decides to play a trick on him and orders his men to take Sly home, dress him in fine clothes and treat him like a nobleman. A band of strolling actors are hired to perform an entertainment. The Lord's pageboy is dressed in women's clothing and told to act as Sly's 'wife'. As the bemused Sly wakes, he is told that he has been deluded for fifteen years and that his old life is a bad dream. The players announce that they will perform a cheerful play to restore his health, and Sly settles down with his 'wife' to watch the show.

## Act I: Two sisters and their suitors

A young man, Lucentio, arrives in Padua with his servant Tranio. They witness an argument that erupts in the street. Baptista is refusing to allow two rivals, elderly Gremio and young Hortensio, to court his daughter Bianca until a husband is found for her elder sister Katherina, who is considered a bad-tempered 'shrew'. Everyone belittles Katherina to her face. The suitors agree to find a husband for her and also to engage tutors for Bianca, in order to curry favour with her father. Lucentio is smitten by Bianca.

Hortensio's friend Petruccio arrives in Padua, seeking a wealthy wife. Undeterred by Hortensio's description of Katherina, he boasts that he will win her. Hortensio accompanies him to Baptista's house disguised as a Latin tutor. Lucentio is heading there too, disguised as a music teacher, while Tranio assumes Lucentio's identity.

## Act II: The marriage market

Katherina bullies Bianca into telling her which suitor she likes better, Gremio or Hortensio. It becomes clear that Bianca is her father's pet. The would-be suitors arrive, and the disguised 'tutors' go off to meet the two sisters. As Petruccio drives his marriage bargain, Hortensio re-enters – Katherina has smashed a lute over his head. Petruccio and Katherina are left alone; they spar and argue, but Petruccio tells her that he will marry her whatever her feelings. He then assures Baptista that the courtship is going splendidly. Gremio and Tranio (disguised as Lucentio) compete for Bianca's hand by boasting of their wealth. Tranio wins, but then realises he must produce Lucentio's father Vincentio to confirm the dowry.

# Act III: Lovers in disguise, and a chaotic wedding

Hortensio and Lucentio, in their tutor disguises, bicker as they instruct Bianca. Lucentio manages to declare his love between scraps of Latin verse. Meanwhile, the guests are ready for the wedding of Petruccio and Katherina, but there is no sign of Petruccio. Katherina is angry and humiliated. He finally arrives, dressed in rags and tatters, and after a 'mad' ceremony (III.2.181) he refuses to attend the wedding feast. Katherina tries to defy him and stay, but he orders his servant Grumio to draw his weapon to 'rescue' her. The guests laugh as Katherina is taken away. Bianca gets the place of honour at the bridal dinner.

# Act IV: Life with Petruccio

Petruccio's servant Grumio describes the journey home, a muddy nightmare. Petruccio rages at the servants non-stop. Katherina tries to intercede, but he ensures she gets no dinner or sleep by complaining that nothing is good enough for her. He then tells us that this is a technique for taming Katherina.

Hortensio, meanwhile, has found himself a rich widow and joins Petruccio at his house. Tranio tricks a merchant into playing the role of Vincentio, and he agrees a dowry with Baptista. Petruccio orders new clothes for Katherina to wear to Bianca's wedding – but he treats the tailor and the milliner with the same bad temper as he does the servants. They set off in their old mudstained clothes – still hungry.

Petruccio refuses to complete their journey back to Padua until Katherina agrees that the sun is really the moon because he says so. Then on their way they meet an old man, and Petruccio orders her to greet the 'gentlewoman'. Katherina does this in style. The puzzled old man proves to be the real Vincentio.

# Act V: Wives and 'shrews'

The real Vincentio encounters Baptista with Tranio (still pretending to be Lucentio) and the Merchant (pretending to be Vincentio), who are concluding the marriage settlement. He is nearly arrested, but just in time Lucentio and Bianca arrive, already married. Katherine and Petruccio decide to stay and see the outcome, but he demands a kiss first.

As everyone shares a feast, the new brides and bridegrooms (Bianca and Lucentio, along with Hortensio and the Widow) mock Petruccio and Katherina's marriage. A wager is declared: each husband will summon his wife. Bianca and the Widow refuse to come; Katherina enters at once and demonstrates her obedience with a speech about wifely duty. Petruccio is delighted, and calls for a kiss, making us wonder who the 'shrew' is now.

We do not know what happens to Christopher Sly.

# INDUCTION 1

## Summary

- Christopher Sly is thrown out of an inn by the Hostess. She demands money for the glasses he has broken. She goes to fetch the authorities. Sly falls asleep.
- A hunting party finds Sly. The Lord gives orders to take him home and dress him in fine clothes. The plan is to tell Sly when he wakes that he is a 'mighty lord' (line 63) who has been 'lunatic' (line 62) for fifteen years.
- Some strolling players enter and are enlisted to provide an entertainment for a nobleman who has 'never heard a play' (line 95).
- The Lord sends a servant to prepare his pageboy Bartholomew to play the role of Sly's noble wife. He leaves to supervise the deception.

## Analysis

This first scene of the Induction introduces a number of themes mirrored in the taming plot.

### Acting and illusion

One important theme is role-playing. The Lord and his servants plan disguises to deceive Sly: later, we watch the male characters in both plot and subplot change clothes and identities to pursue their aims. With the entry of the troupe of players, the layers of illusion become thicker. The actors, who earn their living by deception, are deceived by the Lord, who tells them that Sly is a deluded nobleman. This Induction reminds us continually that we are in a theatre watching pretence and performance. This point is reinforced by the discussion of the role Bartholomew is to play: here is a boy actor playing a male servant playing a lady.

### Images of hunting

The entry of the Lord is signalled by hunting-horns and much technical talk of hounds. This fits another key theme of the play. All the suitors can be seen as fortune-hunters, who are after Baptista's 'treasure' (II.1.32). The Lord implies he has been betting on his hounds, just as the bridegrooms bet on their wives at the end of the play (and with similar sums at stake). Petruccio tells us how he will set about taming Katherina as he might tame a falcon (see **Part Four: Imagery**).

## Progress booster: An actor takes a cue

Look our for echoes and contrasts. In his noblewoman's dress, Bartholomew must curtsey and ask Sly in a gentle voice:

What is't your honour will command
Wherein your lady and your humble wife
May show her duty and make known her love? (lines 114–6)

These lines will be reflected by the transformed Katherina at the end of the play. Bartholomew is performing a role according to his Lord's detailed orders: are we to assume Katherina's feelings are no more 'real' than Bartholomew's love for Sly?

# Study focus: How to play a woman

A **feminist** critic might focus attention on this role of the boy actor. All the male characters have clear views on how women should behave, which conform to the Lord's 'recipe' for instructing Bartholomew. Petruccio treats Katherina's 'shrewish' personality as a kind of illusion which she will eventually drop: he makes extensive use of 'props' and 'costumes' in his 'taming school' (IV.2.55); he adopts an outrageous outfit, rips up Katherina's new clothes and throws things until she understands the part she is to play in his world.

Is the playwright showing us that women's roles and behaviour are not 'natural' but are constructed by the society they live in? Or is he teaching men how to use their power to ensure the behaviour they want from their wives?

## Power and status

The Induction highlights the importance of both social rank and identity. There are a number of power struggles that will be echoed in the main action. Sly sees himself as superior to the Hostess because the Slys are a 'better', more noble family. She asserts herself by threatening him with the 'headborough' (l.10). Both seem confident that they will win the battle.

With the arrival of the Lord, however, we see real social power. Like Petruccio, he expects everyone to accept his version of events and assumes nobody will question them. Just as Petruccio's eccentric behaviour forces not only Katherina but everyone else to accept his version of reality, so the Lord retains the upper hand in the deception. He decides how his servants are to respond to the situation. When Sly is licensed to behave like a lord, he ensures he will be on hand to 'abate the over-merry spleen / Which otherwise would grow into extremes' (lines 136–7). The Lord's power is never questioned on stage. However, Sly is established as a recognisable individual rather than a cartoon drunk. The Lord's deception could be viewed as a cruel abuse of power.

## Language and power

The role of language and its link to power is also suggested in this part of the Induction. Sly's rank and identity are to be transformed and he is to be offered power – but only for a limited period and only as a joke. His noisy, shouting entry links him to Katherina, who begins the main plot making what is characterised by the male Paduans as an infernal din, only to be silenced. Sly will gradually change his language in the next scene, and soon fall silent.

The characters of lesser power in the main plot will do the same. The servants Tranio and Biondello will adopt different roles and language as Lucentio commands, but revert to their former status at the end. Katherina eventually speaks with what many would argue is her husband's voice in the final scene. Her famous final capitulation is perhaps an endorsement of male power and supremacy, just as the trick set up in the Induction is a lord's whim.

**A05 KEY INTERPRETATION**

It is common in modern productions for an actor to double the roles of Petruccio and Christopher Sly. For example, in the 1978 Michael Bogdanov production, Jonathan Pryce and Paola Dionisotti played Sly and the Hostess, and then played Petruccio and Katherina. This underlines some of the parallels set up in the Induction, but of course means that Sly cannot be present on stage throughout.

**A03 KEY CONTEXT**

It is worth noting that in the eighteenth and nineteenth centuries some people thought that Katherina had too many opportunities to speak and actors would boost their roles at her expense. In his version *Catherine and Petruccio* (1754), David Garrick took over Katherina's final speech and turned it into a lecture for him to deliver as Petruccio. The Victorian actor Henry Irving cut most of Katherina's arguments about the sun and moon and replaced them with the line 'I see 'tis useless to resist'.

# EXTRACT ANALYSIS: INDUCTION 1, LINES 1–43

The opening of the Induction gets the play off to a noisy and energetic start, with the eviction of Sly from the tavern. While comic in its own right, the Induction also **foreshadows** events and themes in both the plot and subplot. However, it does not replicate them exactly. Rather, it acts as an **ironic** commentary on them and implies different ways in which the audience might choose to interpret them.

The exchange between Sly and the Hostess, about the drunkard's refusal to accept responsibility for his behaviour and pay for the glasses he has broken, anticipates the sparring of Katherina and Petruccio. It is an opportunity for some rough battle-of-the-sexes physical comedy, familiar in the **farce** convention that Shakespeare draws on here. As such it makes greater use of slapstick than the Katherina-Petruccio altercations – and the Hostess is more successful than Katherina in getting her own way.

Sly's aggressive attitude to women echoes some of the darker aspects of Petruccio. On the other hand, his lack of social power mirrors Katherina's. Both stand up for themselves but have no real social status to protect them. Sly is a low-status 'beggar' (line 40), just as Kate, as a woman, is considered worthless until she conforms. The 'foul and loathsome … image' (line 34) that the tinker presents reflects the way sharp-tongued Katherina is labelled a 'fiend of hell' (I.1.88). It is clear that Sly – like Katherina – will be acted upon by men in authority. The police ('the third borough', line 12) or the Lord's tricks will ensnare him.

Both Sly and Katherina face public humiliation. Sly is threatened with the stocks by the Hostess, and Katherina is frequently embarrassed in public by Petruccio and the other suitors. Nor are Sly and Katherina allowed to exercise their own wills; as the huntsman points out, Sly 'cannot choose' (line 41), and nor can Kate. She is married against her will, her fiery behaviour suppressed.

Sly will be made to believe that he is a lord. The language used to describe the process – 'flatt'ring dream … worthless fancy' (line 43) – suggests a magical transformation. It also implies a spectacle for the Lord's enjoyment. Like Sly, Katherina is bewildered as if in a dream during her taming, and the other characters in the main plot see her metamorphosis into an obedient wife as a 'wonder' (V.2.112). Although Petruccio is serious in his intent, and the Lord is playing a practical joke, Katherina is made into a comic spectacle just as Sly is.

**KEY CONTEXT**   **A03**

Female characters like the Hostess were familiar comic **stereotypes** to Shakespeare and his audience. During his youth Shakespeare would have watched the Biblical Mystery Plays acted out by the community in the larger English towns. (These were later banned.) For example, Noah's wife was shown as a noisy shrew so busy arguing she almost fails to board Noah's Ark in time.

The reactions of the other characters to Katherina's humiliation at the wedding ceremony suggest that Petruccio is providing his Paduan audience with a comic interlude for their entertainment. Gremio says, 'Went they not quickly, I should die with laughing' (III.2.242). His amusement is foreshadowed in this scene of the Induction when the Lord says that he will remain on hand to ensure that the hilarity caused by his tricks does not become too great. Are we invited to assume that the mind games of the Lord and Petruccio are funny because they are played on their social inferiors? Or are we invited to side with the victims?

The Induction is full of technical terms about hunting. The Lord uses these to show off his hounds as a millionaire today might boast about his Porsche (and to assert his social superiority over his servant-huntsman, who may well in fact know more than he does). Ironically, more care is lavished on the hounds than is meted out to Sly and Katherina. When she submits to her husband's authority, Katherina is given the praise that Echo, Merriman and the rest have deserved for their efforts during the hunt.

The pairing off of Clowder with the 'deep-mouth'd brach' (line 17) reflects an important part of the Lord's scheme for deceiving Sly by presenting him with a 'wife'. It may also be a reminder of the brisk way Baptista arranges the matches of his daughters, with an eye to his own convenience rather than theirs. Petruccio is linked to the Lord by his use of hunting imagery, although – perhaps significantly – he will prefer a different sport, hawking. Animal imagery will continue to suggest the natural order of things in this play. It evokes a world in which women are meant to be like tame dogs and falcons, part of their husband's goods and chattels, for men to train and enjoy as and when they please. 'Tomorrow' the Lord intends to go hunting again (line 28); Petruccio will expect his Kate to speak and perform on cue too.

Clothes play an important part in this play, too. The Lord wants Sly to be 'wrapped in sweet clothes' (line 37) and have rings placed on his fingers. Bartholomew will wear a dress. Katherina will be subjected to considerable harassment while being fitted for wedding clothes. Like the Lord, Petruccio will be able to choose what he and his wife wear. This is a sign of his power, as clothes shape identity. Throughout the play, everyone, from Tranio to the Merchant, will find that what you wear affects how you are treated and what you can do. Most of the characters in the play respond to surface appearances.

**A03** **KEY CONTEXT**

In the anonymous play *The Taming of A Shrew*, there is a much fuller working-out of the Christopher Sly plot. You can read Sly's extra scenes – including the ending of the play – at the back of the Arden edition, just as originally printed, or in Stanley Wells and Gary Taylor's edition of Shakespeare's plays, *William Shakespeare: The Complete Works* (1988).

**A03** **KEY CONTEXT**

The Lord generally assumes that his views and desires are paramount. His huntsman is a fool, Sly is a fit object of derision and women are weepy; he later recommends an onion to help the disguised Bartholomew weep real tears. Nobody disputes this with him, but the strolling players might take a dim view of the way he disparages their craft. In other plays, notably *Hamlet*, Shakespeare shows actors as able to weep and to draw tears from others by the power of their playing.

# INDUCTION 2

## Summary

- Sly wakes, calling for beer. The servants pretend not to understand when he talks about his life, telling him he has had a prolonged fit of lunacy.
- With the Lord taking the lead, they offer Sly various pleasures until he begins to believe their story.
- Bartholomew enters as his 'lady'. Sly invites him to bed; he manages to refuse.
- The players enter, and Sly and his 'wife' settle down to watch a comedy.

## Analysis

### Transformation and comedy

In this scene, both Sly and Bartholomew have show-stopping entrances in their new clothes. In Elizabethan England there were strict laws about the colours and fabrics that each social class was permitted to wear. The audience would have been interested in the changes of clothing in this scene on several different levels: as a display of fashion; as a politically rather shocking sight of a tinker in silks; and perhaps also as visual comedy as they watched Sly getting to grips with unfamiliar garments that may fit him very badly.

### Cross-dressing

Gender disguise was a popular device in comedy of the period – Shakespeare used it several times. Bartholomew's dilemma when Sly tries to sleep with him is typical of the comic confusion a playwright could create on this theme. It also **foreshadows** the way Petruccio avoids consummating his marriage – although his reasons are of course more complex.

Bartholomew the page is not really at ease in his female role. The Lord's suggestion that he should carry an onion to help him weep womanly tears indicates a very simplistic approach to the idea of gender disguise. Perhaps the speech the disguised Bartholomew makes to Sly is also performed with comic awkwardness. This may affect the way the audience later responds to Katherina's speech of submission at the end of the play.

## Key quotation: Sly more 'real' than others A01

Come, madam wife, sit by my side
And let the world slip: we shall ne'er be younger. (lines 137–8)

Sly's closing remark shows that he may have been seduced into accepting the Lord's illusions, but also that he is keen to get the most out of the entertainment. His remark that life is short reminds us that he has little time to enjoy the luxuries the Lord takes for granted. It makes him a more human figure than those around him.

## Revision task 1: How important is the Induction? A02

Write notes on the arguments for cutting or retaining the Induction, possibly expanding it with material from other historical texts, or your own material.

# ACT I SCENE 1

## Summary

- Lucentio arrives in Padua with his servant Tranio.
- Baptista refuses to allow Gremio and Hortensio to woo his younger daughter, Bianca, until a husband is found for her elder sister, Katherina.
- Gremio and Hortensio resolve to find Katherina a husband.
- Lucentio falls in love with Bianca and changes clothes with Tranio in order to court her in disguise.
- Sly is bored by what he has seen of the play so far.

## Analysis

### A scene of farce

It is made rapidly clear that we are about to watch an Italian-style, **farcical** comedy. Lucentio, the young lover, his comic servant Tranio, Gremio, the elderly man who wants to marry the pretty girl, and Baptista, the dictatorial father more interested in wealthy matches than the happiness of his daughters, are familiar figures from the ***commedia dell'arte***. All the plays from Italianate comedy like this involved a basic plot: a pair of young lovers overcome a series of obstacles in order to marry, often with the help of a clever servant (see **Part Four: Genre**).

### A different kind of character?

The audience knows what to expect from these characters. However, as soon as Katherina speaks it is obvious that she is not simply a comic obstacle to Bianca's happiness; she is also an individual in her own right. Stereotyped images of the 'shrewish' woman take it for granted, just as the men do here, that she is naturally 'too rough' (line 55), 'wonderful froward' (line 69), and given to 'loud alarums' (line 126).

A link between the shrewish scold and the devil was frequently made in Elizabethan folklore (see **Part Four: Imagery**). However, this scene clearly indicates that there is a cause for Katherina's behaviour. Her father's first words make it clear that she is the unwanted elder daughter. Her accusation that he is making a 'stale' (line 58) of her – a laughing stock – shows how unhappy she is at this public humiliation.

Baptista seems to be parading her as a spectacle for Bianca's suitors to mock. He makes it obvious that he prefers the quiet, apparently obedient Bianca – 'my' Bianca, as he usually calls her. He barely acknowledges Katherina. He speaks as if she were not there, or instructs her to stay outside when he leaves. Katherina is not a valued member of the family unit – quite the reverse. She is a troublesome outsider and a thorn in her father's flesh.

**A03** **KEY CONTEXT**

The stage directions at line 47 reveal that Shakespeare is drawing on *commedia dell'arte* sources. A 'pantaloon' is a stock *commedia* character, a comical old man who lusts after and seeks marriage with a younger woman. In the *commedia* he would have worn a mask, and would have walked with strutting movements like a turkey. We will not expect Gremio to change or develop as a person, and he never does.

**A05** **KEY INTERPRETATION**

In her 1996 edition of the play, the critic Frances Dolan points out that the word 'shrew' is exclusively used of women – there is no exact equivalent to describe a man who talks too much or too rudely (*The Taming of the Shrew*, Bedford Press edition).

### A wicked woman?

The male characters view Katherina as a threat as well as a nuisance. They are scared of her and effectively endorse her father's treatment of her by taunting her. Gremio's remark to Baptista that he would like to 'cart her' (line 55) suggests he would be quite happy for her to suffer even greater shame: 'carting' means the parading of a convicted prostitute or a witch on the way to punishment.

Gremio seems to sum up the masculine view of Katherina when he says it would be a mercy to find someone who would 'thoroughly woo her, wed her, and bed her, and rid the house of her' (lines 143–4). The phrasing here **ironically foreshadows** Petruccio's rough wooing. It clearly indicates that Katherina is seen as a nuisance the men need to be 'rid' of; Tranio's words at line 180 reinforce this idea. The language suggests that in Gremio's – and the other men's – eyes, Katherina is barely human.

### A silent woman?

Katherina's chief 'crime' would seem to be that she speaks out. Lucentio is attracted to Bianca because of her 'silence' (line 70). He considers this quality essential to the 'mild behaviour and sobriety' of an ideal woman. Katherina, on the other hand, makes impatient and spirited retorts to the men's jeers. It is notable that the first thing she does is ask a question. She does not get an answer.

Given the fact that Katherina is outnumbered by men on the stage, all of whom bully her rather than engaging in conversation, she is likely to win the audience's affection for the underdog. However, Katherina speaks less and less as the scene goes on. It may be that Baptista's endless demonstrations that he prefers to 'commune' with Bianca (line 101) wear her down. He does not want Katherina with him, but she cannot really remain alone with the bullying suitors either. Her exit suggests she has given up the struggle to be heard.

Bianca colludes with Baptista in crushing Katherina, 'humbly' subscribing to his 'pleasure', making no demands, taking herself off to study her 'books and instruments' (lines 81–2). This not only flaunts her attractions to the men, but calls attention to the failings of Katherina. We may begin to suspect that Bianca is not as sweet as she appears.

### Power and money

Marriage is firmly linked to money in this scene. It is a financial game played by men. It is men who decide what kind of women are valuable (quiet, pretty ones) and they then compete for them. As the suitors jostle for position, Baptista holds all the cards. A bargain must be struck before they get a chance to court his 'treasure'. Baptista is wily. Gremio and Hortensio not only agree to try to find a husband for Katherina (saving her father the trouble), they also foot the bill for Bianca's education. This daughter is indeed a prize, worth improving so that Baptista can barter her successfully on the marriage market.

On the other hand, it is understood that Baptista will have to provide a large dowry to get Katherina off his hands. Gremio remarks, 'Thinkest thou, Hortensio, though her father be very rich, any man is so very a fool to be married to hell?' (lines 122–4). These lines set up a sense of anticipation. We wonder what the man who takes on Katherina will be like, and what his motives will be.

---

**KEY CONTEXT**

The received wisdom of the period was that woman were naturally given to too much speaking. A popular inn sign was 'The Silent Woman' – a woman with no head.

**KEY CONTEXT**

Male-authored religious tracts in sixteenth-century Italy listed the chief virtues women should possess as: Chastity, Silence, Modesty, Reticence, Sobriety and Obedience. Bianca is looking like a promising catch at this point.

# Study focus: Lucentio, the practical man?

**A02**

Lucentio, lovestruck by a woman he has never spoken to, compares her to classical beauties, and says that, like a courtly lover, he will 'burn … pine … perish' if he does not 'achieve' her (lines 154–5). His servant is more pragmatic and worldly. Tranio has to explain a piece of vital information – the need to find a husband for Katherina – which Lucentio has missed while gazing at Bianca: 'Perhaps you marked not what's the pith of all' (line 165).

It is Tranio who spurs him to action: 'If you love the maid, / Bend thoughts and wits to achieve her' (lines 177–8). Like Hortensio and Gremio, Tranio recognises that one has to work for a prize. Tranio will do much of the work involved in winning Bianca. His line to Lucentio, 'I pray, awake, sir' (line 177), rousing him from a daydream about Bianca, is one of many that suggests Tranio is the real brains of the pair. He fits the **commedia dell'arte** role of the clever servant who helps the young lovers.

## Clever outsiders

Petruccio, the outsider from Verona, will succeed in his 'taming school' (IV.2.55) by outwitting Katherina and the Paduans. Tranio, the outsider from Bergamo, will fool the Paduans, the foreign Merchant and, briefly, Vincentio. By the end of this scene, plot and subplot are interwoven. Deception is the order of the day as Tranio and Lucentio exchange clothes and go on to deceive the slower-witted Biondello as to why. Key dramatic ideas – the importance of role-reversal and transformation, and the deceptiveness of appearances – are established here. This **comedy** has started with some very unromantic bargaining.

# Progress booster: Masters, servants and comedy

**A02**

Consider the relationship between master and man in the subplot. Does Lucentio really think up the idea of disguise by himself, or does Tranio just let him think that he has? Does Lucentio take any initiatives on his own?

**A03** **KEY CONTEXT**

The word 'scold' (line 171) is often used about Katherina – as a verb, which it is here, to describe what she *does*, or as a noun to tell us what she *is*. These days the word 'scold' tends to suggest nothing more dangerous than a telling-off. But a woman in Shakespeare's time could be subjected to severe, even violent punishment. The 'scold's bridle' was a metal brace with a spike that would cut the tongue if the wearer tried to speak.

**A03** **KEY CONTEXT**

Tranio comes from the northern Italian town of Bergamo. Traditionally this was associated with the comic servant characters of the *commedia dell'arte*, who were depicted as poor immigrant outsiders in the more affluent south.

# ACT I SCENE 2

## Summary

- Petruccio arrives in Padua and tells his friend Hortensio that he is seeking a rich wife. Hortensio tells him about Katherina and he decides to go and see her.
- Hortensio disguises himself as a Latin tutor for Bianca, in order to court her.
- Lucentio is already there disguised as Cambio, a music teacher, hired by Gremio. Tranio arrives, disguised as Lucentio.
- Petruccio boasts that he will solve their problems by courting Katherina.

## Analysis

### Comic violence?

The opening argument between Petruccio and his servant Grumio can be interpreted in more than one way. Grumio's apparent confusion about the words 'knock me' (line 8, meaning 'knock for me') is not original, but a very ancient joke. Many of the audience would have seen similar routines at the theatre and might regard it as straightforwardly funny. Or, perhaps, the staleness of the humour might be the point, with Petruccio and Grumio playfully acting out a very old joke for their own amusement. However, the threats of beating and the twisting of Grumio's ears introduce the idea of physical violence. Although the violence here is cartoon-ish, with no real hurt being done, it can cast a shadow over the wooing of Katherina.

### 'I come to wive it wealthily'

We are immediately aware that Petruccio is interested in money; he has 'come abroad' (line 57) to seek his fortune and is breezily unconcerned about the character of his wife-to-be: anyone 'rich enough to be Petruccio's wife' (line 66) will do. Many of his speeches in this scene include references to wealth. By the end of it, the 'hero' is already speaking of Katherina as part of his goods and chattels, as he will on their wedding day.

### Talking

Petruccio outlines his previous life experiences (lines 197–209) in a speech that is not so much a biography as a great burst of energy, a routine for the star of the show. This quality attracts the audience to him even while they may have reservations about his actions. He clearly likes to be centre stage and takes pleasure in playing with words. Over a few lines his language draws on classical literature, martial arts, and domestic tasks like roasting chestnuts.

Rather than being scared of a woman's tongue, like the Paduans, he is confident in his own command of speech. As Grumio remarks, 'scolding would do little good upon him' because 'he begin once, he'll rail in his rope-tricks' (lines 108–11). These lines are a clear indication that Katherina has met her match. Petruccio has decisively established himself as the central character in the play. It is clear that it is the talkers in this play who will triumph.

**KEY INTERPRETATION** **A05**

In Cole Porter's frequently revived 1948 musical *Kiss Me, Kate*, about a theatre company staging *The Taming of the Shrew*, 'I come to wive it wealthily in Padua' (line 74) is the opening line of Petruccio's song. The brash and bouncy style is a good indication of how some of his speeches might be performed.

**KEY INTERPRETATION** **A05**

In Gale Edwards's production for the Royal Shakespeare Company in 1995, Grumio stood behind Petruccio and mimed along to his 'Have I not heard lions roar' speech (lines 197–209): clearly he had heard his master show off in company many times before.

## Key quotation: Smart talking    A01

Following Tranio's persuasive claim to court Bianca, Gremio remarks that, 'this gentleman will out-talk us all' (line 247).

# ACT II SCENE 1

## Summary

- Katherina ties Bianca's hands and torments her to find out which of her suitors she prefers.
- The suitors arrive. Petruccio and the disguised 'tutors' Lucentio and Hortensio introduce themselves.
- Petruccio arranges his marriage bargain. Meanwhile, Katherina breaks a lute over Hortensio's head.
- Left alone together, Katherina and Petruccio argue. He tells her that he will marry her regardless of her objections.
- He tells her father that everything is going splendidly and the men agree that the wedding will take place on Sunday.
- As her suitors bid for Bianca's hand, Tranio wins, but then realises he must provide a 'father' to confirm the large dowry he has offered.

## Analysis

### Sibling rivalry

The first part of this scene shows Katherina at her worst – noisy, resentful of her sister and physically violent. However, the rest of the Minola family also appear in a negative light. Bianca's 'So well I know my duty to my elders' (line 7) sounds smug and sanctimonious, and spitefully underlines Katherina's status as the elder daughter who cannot find a suitor. Baptista's crude description of his eldest daughter, delivered to her face – 'thou hilding of a devilish spirit' (line 26) – is also deeply unkind.

Does Katherina's relentless harassment of the tied-up Bianca on the subject of her suitors suggest that she is envious, that she too would like to be married? While she evidently despises all the men she has met so far (and they are not very impressive) she is clearly unhappy with her present social position. She is afraid that the family will use her unwed status to ensure she is publicly humiliated: 'she must have a husband, / I must dance barefoot on her wedding-day' (lines 32–3).

It is easy to sympathise here with Katherina's desire to 'find occasion of revenge' (line 36). The way in which she interprets female silence in this scene is interesting because it is so different from the men's understanding of it. She says of Bianca that 'her silence flouts me' (line 29) – in other words, it does not spring from the maidenly modesty that Lucentio is so smitten by, but is a sign of passive aggression. (Bianca's behaviour to her new husband at the end of the play suggests that Katherina is correct here.) Katherina's line to her father, just before her exit, suggests that she is worn down by his endless reproaches – 'Talk not to me, I will go sit and weep' (line 35). Yet again, she goes off alone, the family outsider. But Baptista feels that he suffers the most: 'Was ever gentleman thus grieved as I?' (line 37). His line provides Petruccio with the perfect comic entrance, arriving right on cue like the answer to a prayer.

## Revision task 2: Family ties

Each member of the Minola family claims to be the most unhappy. Write notes on each, explaining who, at this point, you think has most reason to be the most unhappy.

---

**A05  KEY INTERPRETATION**

Katherina's line 'And, for your love to her, lead apes in hell' (line 34) is an allusion to the idea that unmarried women were said to lead apes into hell because they had no children. In the 1980 BBC production of the play, directed by Jonathan Miller, Katherina is genuinely upset when she uses the phrase. She screams and cries and throws an apple at her father as she leaves the set.

**A04  KEY CONNECTION**

In Shakespeare's later comedy *Much Ado About Nothing*, the resolutely unmarried Beatrice also talks about 'leading apes into Hell' but in a cheerful spirit. She says that the devil will send her 'away to Saint Peter afore the heavens. He shows me where the bachelors sit, and there live we as merry as the day is long' (Act 1 Scene 3, lines 42–4).

**KEY CONTEXT**  A02

It is interesting to note that Petruccio has 589 lines in *The Taming of the Shrew*; no other character even comes close to this. Tranio, who acts in disguise and organises much of the subplot, has 293, and Katherina has the third largest role at 219 lines.

## The men decide

As usual, the women are offstage while the business of marriage is discussed. The contrast between Katherina's exit and Petruccio's opening remark, 'Pray, have you not a daughter / Called Katherina, fair and virtuous?' (lines 42–3), followed by Baptista's blunt, 'I have a daughter, sir, called Katherina' (line 44), is comic. However, Baptista's response to Petruccio's polite descriptions of Katherina's virtues is to issue a kind of health warning, implying a disturbing contempt for his daughter. The sum he names as her dowry is enormous (about a thousand times the yearly earnings of a tradesman of the period), as if getting rid of her is a priceless gift.

Remarkably, it is left to Petruccio to raise the issue of provision for Katharina if she is widowed. In all this talk of dowries and estates, and Petruccio's abrupt declaration that he cannot come to woo every day, there is no hint of romance. Only Baptista's feeble insistence that Petruccio must obtain Katherina's love suggests that marriage is more than a business transaction. We are not likely to be convinced by Baptista's concern for his daughter's feelings. Nevertheless, the idea of romantic love has, at least, been raised.

## Preparing for battle

Petruccio's boast that he will prove a mountain of strength in the face of Katherina's rage is undercut by the perfect comic timing of Hortensio's entry, *'with his head broke'* (line 141). Petruccio's comment, 'Now, by the world, it is a lusty wench' (line 159) is likely to raise a laugh. It may be spoken **ironically**. But, given that he has heard Hortensio speak rudely of Katherina, Petruccio may not have very much sympathy with his plight. He may instead feel intrigued by the prospect of meeting the woman who has challenged him. The stage is set for a battle of the sexes and the audience will be eagerly anticipating the confrontation.

**KEY INTERPRETATION**  A05

The actress Fiona Shaw, who played Katherina in Jonathan Miller's production for the Royal Shakespeare Company in 1987, comments, 'She comes in – and is *talked* to by a man for the first time; that's what disorientates her. Not his violence, but his gentleness.' (See Carol Rutter, *Clamorous Voices: Shakespeare's Women Today*, The Women's Press, 1988.)

However, the battle is not staged on equal terms. Petruccio confides his strategy directly to the audience. This confirms his place as the central figure of the play. Katherina is never given a **soliloquy**. From now on, she will react to Petruccio rather than take the dramatic initiative. Petruccio's speech suggests a bright confidence about his prospects and about the methods he will use to 'woo her with some spirit' (line 168). While Bianca's suitors want to 'cart' Katherina, or lock her up, Petruccio expects his words to prevail. He will 'out talk' Katherina: the word 'say' appears five times, and there are eight other verbs describing speaking in this one speech. The accomplished performer we have already seen showing off to the men is preparing his role as wooer.

# Study focus: A complex episode

The scene between Katherina and Petruccio has been interpreted very diversely. One critic, J. D. Huston, called Petruccio's behaviour 'psychological rape'. It has also been perceived as subtle and even gentle. There are sections of the text to support both readings, as if the playwright is uncertain whether his play is about a swashbuckling shrew-tamer from traditional folklore, or a witty couple coming to care for each other. It is for the actors, or the reader, to decide how the whole should be presented – but this will inevitably mean that some parts of the play are stressed at the expense of others.

## Getting acquainted

Petruccio's familiar and repeated use of the name 'Kate' is an assertion of power. Right from the outset he is claiming the authority to define his chosen bride. Despite her statement that 'they call me Katherine', he persists, culminating in his declaration that she is to be brought 'from a wild Kate to a Kate / Conformable as other household Kates' (lines 279–80). Note that he does not tell her his own name, simply announcing self-importantly, 'Myself am moved to woo thee for my wife' (line 193) thus leaving her at a disadvantage. However, the pair also engage in a more equal kind of conversation, a quick-fire exchange of puns, jokes and insults. Some of these jokes may be obscure to a modern audience, but the brisk and snappy rhythms make it clear that this is a competition to get the last word, and they are both absorbed in it.

## A turning point

But then Petruccio oversteps the mark and makes a joke that is obscene rather than mildly bawdy. Is Katherina insulted by this? It is at this point that she strikes him. His response, 'I swear I'll cuff you, if you strike again' (line 222) could be a straightforward demonstration of superior strength. However, this is the third time that Katherina has struck somebody. Petruccio may be pointing out that he is not prepared to accept the same treatment as passive Bianca and Hortensio the 'tutor'. From this point, neither of them strikes the other. Nor does Petruccio makes any more lewd jokes at Katherina's expense. Without speaking directly about it, the pair seem to have agreed some ground rules.

## Study focus: Language and power

**(A02)**

You may find it useful to look at some of the exchanges of language as power struggles, and decide who wins which exchange.

Petruccio knows how to deliver the conventional praise of virtue and beauty expected of a wooer, but, as he explains in his soliloquy, this is a strategy to confuse the raging Katherina rather than a romantic overture. However, more than once the text indicates a pause before and after a line of praise, for example '– / Thy beauty which doth make me like thee well –' (line 276) which suggests that he is also taken aback by his interest in this woman. Katherina's most effective crushing remark is, 'Where did you study all this goodly speech?' (line 264). She has learnt something about Petruccio – that it takes effort to sustain the personality he is so busily asserting.

## Silence

Any chance of an equal contest is lost as Petruccio moves on to 'plain terms': 'your father hath consented / That you shall be my wife; your dowry 'greed on, / And will you, nill you, I will marry you' (lines 271–3). His force and assurance demonstrate his determination to have things his way. It is interesting, however, that he adds, 'I am a husband for your turn' (line 274). This is perhaps an acknowledgement that Katherina might have needs of her own. Like the early allusion to the need to obtain Katherina's 'love', there may be a hint to the audience that we should see these two as a good match. But Katherina is silent. There is no answer she can give. This is not a proposal, but a display of power. Despite the flashes of attraction and excitement in this courtship, its outcome is a foregone conclusion.

## Petruccio's victory

Petruccio has the power to assert his own view of reality, not just over Katherina but over the unimaginative Paduans. There is no proof that his daughter looks favourably on her perverse suitor, but Baptista happily accepts his story that Petruccio and Katherina have agreed that she will continue to be a 'shrew' in public – 'curst in company' (line 309). This, of course, undermines everything she has to say and renders her powerless. The stage direction *'Exeunt Petruccio and Katherina'* (line 328) does not indicate whether they leave separately or together – an interesting choice for the actors to make.

## Romance and money

Altogether, it is impossible to imagine a less romantic wooing than the meeting of Petruccio and Katherina. But if Petruccio's language and behaviour are outrageous, and sometimes shocking in the focus on money, that of Bianca's suitors is arguably worse. She is effectively auctioned off in a frenzy of bidding. This involves laughably fabulous sums. The men compete so furiously that Bianca is almost forgotten. Gremio, in particular, loses all dignity. His shrill threats to the younger man create comedy for the audience. The ever more wildly exaggerated references to cattle, houses, treasure, ships and land which the two suitors hurl at each other almost take on the status of weapons. 'What, have I choked you with an argosy?' crows Gremio (line 380), leaving us with a vivid comic image of Tranio with a ship half way down his throat.

Tranio, of course, will not be paying for any of his extravagant bids, and is free to enjoy himself in his millionaire disguise. He proves himself almost as adept as Petruccio in controlling people through words. However, Baptista's single-minded focus on money would probably shock the Elizabethan audience, even though they were accustomed to bargaining over marriage contracts. Katherina's sarcastic words, 'You have showed a tender fatherly regard' (line 289), are just as apt from the point of view of his younger daughter. Despite all his loving words to Bianca, this father is content for her to marry the highest bidder. He is even careful to keep another suitor in reserve in case the promised money does not materialise. At the end of this scene her fate is still uncertain, and it is no surprise when Bianca chooses to take matters into her own hands.

# ACT III SCENE 1

## Summary

- Disguised as the tutors 'Cambio' and 'Licio', Lucentio and Hortensio woo Bianca.
- Lucentio reveals his identity in a 'Latin lesson' and declares his love.
- Hortensio gives a 'music lesson' with the same purpose.
- Rejected by Bianca, Hortensio suspects that she is in love with Lucentio.
- Bianca is told to prepare for Katherina's wedding.

## Analysis

### A woman in control?

The wooing of Bianca is in sharp contrast to the wooing of Katherina. Here, the men do not really have the upper hand. Their attempts to assert superiority over each other are comic. Both try to imitate learned scholars, but the effect is of two schoolboys squabbling over their homework. There are clear signs that the modest little maiden they both idealise actually possesses a strong will. Her first two lines suggest that she is someone who makes her own decisions: 'Why, gentlemen, you do me double wrong / To strive for that which resteth in my choice' (lines 16–7). We begin to suspect that the goddess they see is not the real Bianca.

### Courtly love

The love games in this scene are highly conventional, typical of courtly behaviour which would require a woman to be cold and unattainable and a lover to persist despite this. The scene offers the three actors opportunities to shine. They can show off their skills in speaking Latin verse, with 'Cambio's' lesson, and in singing the 'gamut of Hortensio' (line 70), which is a kind of musical game like the song *Do-re-mi* and which would allow for some spirited variations.

However, none of this elegant behaviour allows the characters to learn anything about one another. Bianca is going through the motions of conventional courtship, one moment asserting that, 'In time I may believe, yet I mistrust' (line 49) and almost immediately adding coyly, 'I must believe my master' (line 52). Those among Shakespeare's audience who had a classical education like his own would note another comic aspect: it is absurd that the lovelorn Lucentio should attempt to woo Bianca with Ovid's poetry – essentially a volume of cynical advice on seduction.

## Study focus: Love and disguise **A02**

It seems that Shakespeare is intent on undermining traditional notions of romance in this play. There are very few moments when Bianca and Lucentio are having a real conversation rather than playing verbal games. It is as if they are acting the part of lovers, rather than being in love. Hortensio is spectacularly unromantic. Suspecting he is not Bianca's favourite, he promptly decides that she is not good enough for him – if she prefers the poor tutor to his own charms, it must be because she casts her 'wandering eyes on every stale' (line 88).

**A03** **KEY CONTEXT**

Actors in the Elizabethan companies were expected to be able to play several instruments to a high standard. In the right hands, Hortensio's bumbling with the lute as he is repeatedly accused of being out of tune could provide amusing background music, as a kind of commentary on Lucentio's wooing.

**A04** **KEY CONNECTION**

In many of Shakespeare's later comedies, such as *As You Like It*, disguise is a way for people in love to learn about each other and to see the loved one at his or her least 'romantic'. In *The Taming of the Shrew*, disguise covers the real self.

# ACT III SCENE 2

## Summary

- It is the wedding day, but Petruccio is late. Katherina is angry and hurt.
- He arrives in shabby clothes and rushes everyone off to church.
- Lucentio and Tranio plot to find a 'father' to further the courtship.
- Petruccio refuses to let Katherina attend her own bridal dinner and hurries her away.

## Analysis

### Left at the altar?

The audience is likely to sympathise with Katherina. Her 'shrewishness' in this situation is little more than the voicing of understandably angry feelings as she waits for her 'merry man' (line 14) to arrive and claim her. Her anxiety may suggest that she has a real desire to fit into her social group – who are now witnessing yet another example of her failure to do so by finding an eager bridegroom. Now she has been presented with a man who will take her on, she would, perhaps, like to be married. Certainly, she continues to dread social disgrace and is in tears at the prospect. It is interesting, though, that Katherina suspects Petruccio is 'Hiding his bitter jests in blunt behaviour' (line 13) as a practical joke. She may be wrong about his reasons, but she is the only person in Padua who seems to be aware of the actor in Petruccio.

### Comedy of outrage

The scene continues in a spirit of high **farce**. It offers a major comic opportunity for the actor playing Biondello. This character does not normally appear to be very bright, but faced with a subject he understands, like horses, he becomes ridiculously articulate in a dazzling display of technical terms. Although in a different spirit from the guests' earlier expressions of anxiety about the bridegroom's lateness, his speech has the same function – to create suspense around Petruccio. How will he behave? What will he say? After the rough wooing, we do not expect the wedding to pass off peacefully.

We are not disappointed. Petruccio offers an absurd visual spectacle as soon as he strides on. So that we do not miss the sensation his garments cause, he promptly asks why everyone is staring as if they saw 'Some comet' (line 95). And if his clothes are comic, so too is the puzzlement of the Paduans. While Katherina has had a chance to observe Petruccio in swaggering, boisterous mode when they were alone together, this is a side of him Baptista and the rest have not seen before. Now they find themselves as passive in the face of a dominant male as they have wanted Katherina to be. It is through their eyes, especially Gremio's, that we see the wedding itself. Shakespeare sacrifices what might be thought of as a comic opportunity here; but Petruccio's swearing and violent attack on the priest would have been considered near-blasphemous and not fit to be represented on stage.

**KEY CONTEXT** A03

Although there was a large proportion of unmarried women in Shakespeare's England, documents such as *The Lawe's Resolution of Women's Rights* assumed that all women were 'either married or to be married' rather than having an independent legal status. It is in Katherina's interest to have a husband, as she probably realises.

**KEY INTERPRETATION** A05

Film directors have often decided to show the wedding scene between Petruccio and Katherina. In Franco Zeffirelli's 1967 film, Elizabeth Taylor as Katherina attempts to shout 'I will not' when asked if she will take Petruccio as her husband. Petruccio (Richard Burton) kisses her forcefully just after the word 'will'.

## Key quotation: Real or disguise? A01

'To me she's married, not unto my clothes' (line 116): Petruccio says this in the presence of Tranio, pretending to be Lucentio, Biondello, pretending to be Tranio, and Lucentio, pretending to be a tutor. Perhaps he implies that his relationship with Katherina is 'real' in a way that Bianca's romance is not.

## Petruccio in charge

We now get our first chance to see Katherina and Petruccio as a married couple. After the shocks of Petruccio's initial appearance in this scene, their entrance is surprisingly quiet and polite. From the courtship onwards Petruccio has been in control of events, and this extract confirms that his authority is unquestioned. He refuses to stay for the wedding feast – politely but with increasing force, going from 'It may not be' to 'It cannot be' (lines 198–200). When Katherina, perhaps testing out her power over him as his chosen companion, repeats the host's invitation to stay, it seems that the wife-taming has begun in earnest. Petruccio seems to be going out of his way to humiliate her, forcing her to question him so that he can put her in her place and remind her that she must get used to the idea of asking for his consent and approval: 'I am content you shall entreat me stay' (line 203). When she again asks him to stay, he is perhaps at his most unkind.

Katherina tentatively uses the word 'love' for the first time in speaking to him (line 204) – surely a big step for her – and he ignores her completely and calls for his horse. It is only then that she attempts to assert herself in her longest and most energetic speech for many lines – to find that he refuses to engage with her on equal terms. Rather, Petruccio speaks like the mildest of henpecked husbands – 'O Kate, content thee; prithee be not angry' (line 216) – but continues to do exactly as he likes.

## Study focus: Petruccio's motive

**A02**

Why does Petruccio don the ridiculous clothes and why won't he stay for the feast? Essentially, Petruccio has made a farce of his wedding to show his wife that she must conform or continue to suffer humiliations like these. He acts out the chaos that 'shrewish' behaviour can inflict: disrupting social occasions like feasts and even undermining the solemnity of religion. He wants to shame her into submission by being even more perverse and difficult than she is. By being a 'shrew', Petruccio shows Katherina that it is useless to resist the authority of the dominant male. He can and will shout louder and longer. Until she behaves in the way society expects of women, she will not be allowed to join in its rituals. When she does conform, Katherina will be allowed to attend the feast. As yet, Petruccio does not feel there is anything to celebrate.

## Progress booster: The last word

**A02**

Petruccio's final lines in the scene underline the idea that the male has the right to define the female. Katherina is defined as a piece of Petruccio's property, passed from one owner (her father) to another (her husband). This is a bald statement about male and female power – but if you look through other scenes you can detect the same assumption underlying the men's speeches, for instance in the auction of Bianca, and the wager on wives in the final scene of the play.

**A03** KEY CONTEXT

It has been suggested that Petruccio's choice of outfit in this scene is the kind of costume worn in the ***commedia dell'arte*** by one of the stock characters – the Captain, a boastful soldier given to macho posturing. Petruccio may be making fun of the dominant masculinity he assumes in this scene: the Captain is often a coward at heart.

**A01** PROGRESS BOOSTER

To improve your grade, ensure that you are able to use literary and theatrical terminology, such as **irony** and **farce**. If in the exam you do not feel confident about a term, clearly identify in your own way the particular skill the playwright is using – perhaps 'precise description' or 'physical comedy'.

# EXTRACT ANALYSIS: III.2.190–234

In this scene Petruccio the bridegroom, fresh from the church, loses no time in showing what he expects of Katherina – while leaving her confused and at a loss. He praises her for the qualities he intends her to have in the future as his 'patient, sweet, and virtuous wife' (line 194). Yet when she makes some attempt to show these qualities, asking him to stay to the dinner with a politeness we have not seen before from her, he snubs her mercilessly.

The language games Petruccio plays around the word 'content' are intended to irritate. They undermine her painfully acquired grace of manner and return Katherina to her former fiery self. He allows her the power to tell the guests to go forward to the wedding feast – 'They shall go forward, Kate, at thy command' (line 223) – only to hijack the meaning of that command by preventing her from going with them. His wordplay emphasises how precise her obedience will have to be to 'content' Petruccio. He expects his orders to be followed in a very literal sense. He makes it clear that he has married her on his own terms, and will do as he pleases because as a man he possesses all the power. By the end of the scene this fact will be brought home to Katherina with all the authority of the Bible behind it.

However, it is quite different when Petruccio is speaking to the Paduans. They are all treating the wedding as a Punch and Judy show for their enjoyment. From Gremio's assertion after Katherina's outburst that 'now it begins to work' (line 219) to Bianca's smug 'being mad herself, she's madly mated' (line 245), it is clear that they expect the marriage to be a disaster – and find the idea funny. Petruccio never disparages Katherina to them. He never refers to her dowry or suggests that she is not a desirable match. Rather, he ranges both his wife and himself against the wedding party.

He absolutely refuses to conform to society's expectations of a bridegroom (just as Katherina is an unconventional bride). He does not show any of the respect he displayed to Baptista earlier, issuing a casual invitation to the guests to 'Dine with my father' [in law] (line 195) – presumably at Baptista's expense. He seems, in

some ways, quite puritanical. The way he flaunts his tattered outfit and insists on the distinction between a man and his clothing is very different from the fuss Bianca's suitors make about material goods as they vie for her hand. He also seems to sneer at the wedding feast, as if the guests cannot be trusted to stay sober: 'Carouse full measure to her maidenhead, / Be mad and merry, or go hang yourselves' (lines 226–7).

Although Katherina has a difficult time in this scene, Petruccio's conduct has some gratifying moments for her. The Paduans have sneered at her and Petruccio alike, labelling them 'devil' (lines 154–5). Petruccio addresses them in language very like Katherina's in the previous Act. If he won't give her a chance to speak, at least she can agree with some of his sentiments.

The exit of Katherina and Petruccio repays close attention because it works on so many different levels. It is clearly designed to be full of noisy, bustling physical comedy, but exactly how the actors choose to play this will have an impact on how we understand Petruccio's speech.

It is quite common for Petruccio to be shown carrying Katherina off over his shoulder like a parcel. Certainly her departure isn't meant to be very dignified. But he is creating a more interesting fantasy than that, in a lively speech that effectively silences the onlookers. He pretends that they are trying to steal his bride and defends Katherina with spirit like a knight of chivalry – perhaps even brandishing a weapon. His language reflects the discussion between Lucentio and Tranio earlier in the scene, in which Lucentio resolves to 'steal our marriage' (line 139). Instead of an arranged marriage for financial gain, Petruccio and Katherina's wedding is transformed into an exciting elopement – or, perhaps, a deliberately unromantic parody of Lucentio's courtly-love antics. The audience is more likely to laugh at the amazed wedding guests than at Katherina herself.

Katherina has nothing to say at this point. Is she simply stunned? Or does Petruccio silence her with 'look not big, nor stamp, nor stare, nor fret' (line 229)? She has done most of these things, so the command might be addressed to her. Equally, though, it might be spoken to the rest of the wedding party. It is to them that Petruccio speaks some lines that have become notorious for their misogynistic overtones:

> She is my goods, my chattels; she is my house,
> My household-stuff, my field, my barn,
> My horse, my ox, my ass, my anything (lines 230–2)

Katherina can be in no doubt that she is her husband's property to do with as he pleases, and that she has no choice in the matter. But at least he does not shame her by delivering the lesson right in her face. Rather, it forms part of his fantasy that the Paduans want Katherina for themselves. His list of property is a direct reference to the Bible. The Ten Commandments specifically forbid anyone to 'covet thy neighbour's house … thy neighbour's wife … nor his ox, nor his ass, nor anything that is thy neighbour's' (Exodus 20.17). Although she is labelled as a piece of property, Katherina is at least assumed here to be 'covetable' – desirable property – not the unmarriageable woman taunted by Bianca's suitors, or the unwanted daughter whose father pays to have her removed like household waste.

 **A05** **KEY INTERPRETATION**

In Jonathan Miller's production for the Royal Shakespeare Company in 1987, Brian Cox as Petruccio handed Katherina a Bible during his last speech in this scene. Fiona Shaw, who played Katherina, comments, 'I flick through this … and it dawns on me, this is what I've inherited as an Elizabethan woman.' (Carol Rutter, *Clamorous Voices: Shakespeare's Women Today*, The Women's Press, 1988).

## Key quotation: Petruccio on marriage    **A01**

Petruccio asserts, 'I will be master of what is mine own' (line 230). As far as he is concerned this is the basis of his understanding of marriage. As with some of his other statements on the subject, he seems to be addressing it partly to Katherina, but also to those around him.

# ACT IV SCENE 1

## Summary

- Grumio arrives ahead of Katherina and Petruccio to prepare the house. He tells the servants about their terrible journey in the mud.
- Petruccio enters with Katherina, immediately complains that the food is not good enough and is rude to the servants. She gets nothing to eat.
- He takes Katherina to the bridal chamber and preaches to her about abstinence.
- He explains to the audience that he intends to keep her awake and hungry to tame her as he would a hawk.

## Analysis

### A difficult journey

As in the previous scene, Petruccio's entrance is built up with a piece of description that offers an opportunity for the company's comedian to perform. Grumio – evidently a small man, a 'little pot' (line 5) – shares a double act with the less lively Curtis, with some of the comic violence that featured in his earlier scene with Petruccio. As before, it is possible to interpret the 'lend thine ear' joke (lines 53–5) as a standard comedy routine. Again, though, in this context there can be some troubling overtones. Katherina is too complex a character for any possibility of violence against her to be taken in the same spirit. Grumio's account of her painful journey will almost certainly involve the actor in performing a comic impression of it for Curtis. As a routine for a comic actor this can be played for laughs – but we might also wonder whether Petruccio's treatment of Katherina is out of proportion for the 'crime' of 'shrewish' behaviour.

### Domestic order

During this first sight of Petruccio's house, the servants show a clear grasp of domestic tasks. We are being given a sense of how a household should be – efficient, warm and welcoming to travellers coming in from the cold, like Grumio, who feels reduced to 'a piece of ice' (line 12). This prepares the audience for the domestic chaos Petruccio will create as part of his taming strategy of being 'more shrew' than Katherina (line 76). From the outset, his language is abusive and his behaviour violent. The large number of servants adds to the chaos as boots, water and meat evidently fly through the air.

### Katherina's response

Grumio's first speeches and the short exchange between the servants – 'He kills her in her own humour' (line 169) – indicate that they are colluding with Petruccio to create as much disorder as possible to mirror Katherina's own turbulent personality. Potentially this scene is full of slapstick comedy. But Katherina's silence suggests that her spirit is already breaking. She demands nothing for herself. She addresses her husband with the formal word 'you' rather than the intimate 'thee' he uses to her. We might wonder whether she is afraid to provoke him with her usual kind of speech.

**KEY CONTEXT** **A03**

Grumio's account of the trip home, with its references to horses, would not surprise Shakespeare's audience. References to horses were a standard component of English folklore about wayward women. Many folk tales featured wedding trips home on horseback.

**KEY CONTEXT** **A03**

It has been suggested that the names of the servants in this part of *The Taming of the Shrew* are the names of the actors who played them. Shakespeare would have had a clear idea of how these roles would be performed and how to make the most of features like the Grumio actor's small stature.

However, the woman who hit a servant in Act II now tries to speak up when Petruccio does the same thing. Katherina's sense of justice is reaching out to others. Though he retains his rowdy manner, Petruccio makes a small gesture towards equality at this point. Still making sure she gets no dinner, he links the two of them together in hunger, saying that overdone meat is unhealthy because it nourishes anger and that they should go without because they are both angry people – 'of ourselves, ourselves are choleric' (line 163).

## Study focus: A theory of taming

Curtis offers a clue to the way Shakespeare expects the actor playing Katherina to perform this scene –'as one new risen from a dream' (line 175). The violence and chaos are a nightmare Petruccio is staging for her, just as the Lord of the Induction makes a dream of luxury for Sly. Her world is so changed that she is too puzzled to keep to her usual style of behaviour. Petruccio goes on to enlighten the audience with a **soliloquy** full of the language of hawking. Katherina is described as a falcon, a 'haggard' who must learn to 'come and know her keeper's call' (lines 182–3). This is not simply a **metaphor**. Petruccio is treating his wife exactly as a falconer tames his bird: keeping it hungry and preventing it from sleeping, until it learns to eat from his hand.

This is a tough process which depends on both falconer and bird going through it together. We have some sense of how Katherina feels about it. We know less about what is going on inside Petruccio's mind. He speaks in quite a detached way – a lecture on masculine domination rather than confidences about a specific relationship. He expresses neither love nor dislike for Katherina. Nor does he give any kind of indication that the taming process causes this 'falconer' any discomfort. It is this apparent invulnerability that makes the taming process so uncomfortable to watch – although the actor, if he chooses, may show vulnerability and exhaustion here in his delivery of the lines.

### Katherina's consent

Petruccio preaches a 'sermon of continency' to Katherina (line 172) and goes on to throw the bed into disorder, saying it has not been properly made. Like the neat evasions of Bartholomew in the Induction, this makes it clear to the audience that there will be no sexual activity. This would disturb the temporary nature of the dream states Petruccio and the Lord have created. It sets a boundary: Katherina will at least have a measure of consent around the consummation of the marriage. Petruccio wilfully misunderstands her many times, but never allows a sexual situation to arise where he pretends that 'no' means 'yes'.

## Key quotation: Understanding Petruccio's motivation

Part of the fantasy Petruccio creates is that 'all is done in reverend care' of Katherina (line 193). While this can be seen as cruel mockery, it also allows the possibility of change – the derogatory labels inflicted on her by the other men in the play do not. Perhaps Petruccio knows that, if he can make her change, this 'reverend care' can become real?

**A05** KEY INTERPRETATION

In Jonathan Miller's 1980 BBC production, the audience is encouraged to feel some sympathy for John Cleese as Petruccio during his soliloquy about wife-taming. It is delivered in a weary tone, as he sits quietly at the kitchen table. He yawns and rubs his eyes. He too is suffering, and is not simply a calculating sadist.

# ACT IV SCENE 2

## Summary

- Still disguised as Lucentio, Tranio shows Hortensio the romance developing between Bianca and her 'tutor'. They both renounce her.
- Hortensio reveals his identity and decides to marry a wealthy widow who likes him.
- Tranio and Biondello bamboozle a merchant into playing the part of Vincentio, Lucentio's father.

## Analysis

### Advancing the action

Disguises come thick and fast and deceptions multiply, as the subplot begins to link more closely to the main plot. The action is driven by two deceivers: Bianca, firmly in control of her own fate, and Tranio, as deft in controlling characters and events as Petruccio is.

Hortensio's transformation from adoration to peevish spite is comic. Suddenly his beloved is 'unworthy all the former favours' (line 30). Tranio fans the flames by condemning Bianca for 'lightness' (line 24) – that is, infidelity, although she has of course made no commitment to either of them. This clearly entertains Bianca. Of all the figures in the subplot, Bianca and Tranio get the greatest pleasure from deception. Bianca even briefly allows Tranio to flirt with her (lines 45–9), a sign of their mutual enjoyment of the game.

### Petruccio – a role model?

Hortensio continues to think of himself as a reward for some lucky woman, deciding (without consulting her) to marry the wealthy widow for her 'kindness' (line 41). The references to Petruccio in this scene reinforce his status as 'hero'; it seems that his fame is spreading far and wide as a woman-tamer. Hortensio's urge to marry suddenly and wealthily suggests he would like to be Petruccio – though his giddiness in this scene suggests he could never match Petruccio's single-mindedness. As more couples move closer to marriage, we are being invited to draw comparisons between the pairings.

### A new comic character

Lucentio would clearly be lost without his cunning and helpful Tranio. The duping of the Merchant offers another chance for the Tranio actor to display his comic energy as a fast-talking con-man. Some versions of the play describe the Merchant as a 'pedant'. This may be a clue to how he should be played. A 'pedant' was a well-known comic stereotype, a peevish but learned old man. He may be quite shabby, as Tranio instantly offers him a change of clothing. Yet another character is about to appear in disguise.

**KEY CONNECTION** A04

Eavesdropping scenes like this, where a lover learns something about the beloved – usually something they don't want to know – feature in many comedies of the sixteenth and seventeenth centuries. For example, in Act III Scene 1 of Aphra Behn's *The Rover*, Helena eavesdrops with female companions and learns that Willmore is unfaithful to her. The shape of the stage can allow the audience to watch the reactions of both groups of people simultaneously, while preserving the convention that they cannot see each other.

**KEY CONNECTION** A04

The relationship between a rather slow-witted master and his clever servant has been the basis of many comic novels and plays. The witty butler Lane, in Oscar Wilde's *The Importance of Being Earnest*, does not organise intrigues like Tranio, but his comments on his master's household and love life are very astute.

# ACT IV SCENE 3

## Summary

- A dejected Katherina asks Grumio for food. He teases her with it but does not give her any.
- Petruccio arrives with meat, but a tailor and haberdasher arrive and she has to try on clothes, which he promptly ridicules.
- He announces that they will leave for Baptista's house, but then refuses to move until she agrees with him as to what time of day it is.

## Analysis

### A low point for Katherina

One difficulty in deciding how this scene should be played is that we are not told exactly how much time has elapsed since the wedding. Katherina is exhausted and extremely hungry – but it is not clear whether she has merely missed a meal or two, or whether Petruccio has taken his taming strategy to the point of abuse – Katherina may well be disorientated as a result of starvation and sleep-deprivation.

Katherina is challenged no less than three times in this scene: over food, over clothes, and finally over her husband's right never to be contradicted for his most absurd statements. All the men in the scene seem to collude in tormenting her. Her first speech, although addressed to Grumio, is more like a soliloquy as she tries to make sense of her situation – is Petruccio acting out of spite? She seems to have lost all confidence in her capacity to interpret events for herself.

### Clothing and respectability

The episode with the tailor is full of slapstick and quick-witted verbal comedy. Petruccio excels at elaborate insults and here he is let loose on the fashions of the time – a popular theme for Elizabethan comedy, perhaps underlined here by rough treatment of the gown and its fancy decoration.

The arguments over the clothes also reflect the play's theme of appearance and reality. Does Katherina secretly (or even subconsciously) want to fit in to her society and dress like a respectable wife? Petruccio spells out the cost of wearing a 'gentlewoman's' cap clearly: 'When you are gentle, you shall have one too' (line 73). His lecture to her on how 'honour peereth in the meanest habit' (line 173) recalls his Puritanical assertion at the wedding that the man is more important than his clothing. It rather contradicts his point that Katherina is not ready for the cap of a gentlewoman – but we are used to paradoxes from Petruccio.

### Key quotation: Katherina tries to explain   **A01**

One of the most troubling moments in the play is Katherina's impassioned assertion, 'My tongue will tell the anger of my heart / Or else my heart concealing it will break' (lines 79–80), during her speech when she is going to try on the clothes. Petruccio pretends not to hear, and may well get a laugh for his irrelevant reply – but Katherina has a point. To be perpetually silenced can cause real harm. Our response to the ending of the play will depend to a great extent on how far we consider she is free to speak.

**A04** **KEY CONNECTION**

Katherina's reflections on Petruccio's household suggest an image of what an ideal house should be. You can find a detailed description of such a place in a poem by Shakespeare's contemporary Ben Jonson, *To Penshurst*, which reflects a similar concern for the poor as well as domestic order and hospitality in a house:

'Where comes no guest but is allowed to eat,

Without his fear, and of thy lord's own meat.'

**A05** **KEY INTERPRETATION**

There is an interesting discussion of the role and significance of clothing by Graham Holderness in 'Text and Performance: *The Taming of the Shrew*' in *Shakespeare in Performance*, 2000.

# ACT IV SCENE 4

## Summary

- Tranio and Biondello arrange a meeting between Baptista and the Merchant in his disguise as Vincentio.
- Biondello lets Lucentio know that Baptista is busy with the Merchant and that he can proceed with his secret wedding to Bianca.

## Analysis

### More levels of disguise

Katherina and Petruccio have just left the stage after his lecture on the unimportance of clothes. Their own outfits reflect this attitude; he may well be wearing his eccentric wedding clothes and she may still show signs of her muddy trip to his house. They are replaced at once by a group of people wearing garments that do not belong to them – Tranio as Lucentio, Biondello as Tranio, and the Merchant as Vincentio.

Tranio acts in this scene like a stage manager, bringing all the right people together and directing Lucentio's actions. There is **dramatic irony** in the fact that Baptista agrees to marry Bianca to 'Lucentio', commenting that the young people seem to be very much in love, 'Or both dissemble deeply their affections' (line 41). He unwittingly speaks the truth, having been completely taken in by the wily youngsters.

### Who is deceived?

Lucentio is rather slow-witted. Having failed to pick up Tranio's broad hints, he needs Biondello to explain to him what is happening. In contrast to the force of Petruccio's speeches before and after his wedding, he sounds passive: 'I may and will, if she be so contented' (line 101). We might also feel that there is a hint of danger in his subsequent question: 'She will be pleas'd, then wherefore should I doubt?'

He is just as deluded as Baptista, fondly believing that he has obtained an obedient wife. Significantly, Lucentio ends the scene by speaking of himself as 'Cambio', his assumed name. So much role-play has been going on that neither he nor Bianca can have much idea of the real nature of their chosen partner.

The theme of children who want to marry against the wishes of their parents features in many of Shakespeare plays. Alan Sinfield suggests that such stories were popular because they helped people to think through an actual change in the culture of marriage – and that they continued to be told right into the nineteenth century, when for most people in Britain the arranged marriage largely ceased to exist. (*Faultlines*, OUP, 1992)

Barbara Hodgdon's article 'Bride-ing the Shrew; Costumes that Matter' (*Shakespeare Survey*, 60, 2007) gives a vivid account of the kind of clothing that Katherina and Bianca might be expected to wear in Shakespeare's time.

## Key quotation: Understanding Lucentio

When Biondello is seeking to explain the situation to Lucentio, he summarises it by saying, 'Baptista is safe, talking with the deceiving father of a deceitful son' (lines 81–2). In this context the word 'deceiving'/'deceitful' may mean nothing more than 'pretended'. However, it may also have some moral connotations. Do you think this might also be a comment on Lucentio's actions? He has never attempted to be honest with his father or Baptista.

# ACT IV SCENE 5

## Summary

- Petruccio will not begin their journey to Bianca's wedding until Katherina agrees with him that the sun is the moon.
- They meet Vincentio. Petruccio orders Katherina to greet him as a young girl – and then scolds her. She apologises for her 'mad' mistake.
- Petruccio tells Vincentio about his son's marriage.

## Analysis

### Obedience?

Although this scene appears to be a continuation of Scene 3, the tone of it is different. Something has changed for Katherina. It is possible for an actor to play her as so dazed and disorientated that she no longer trusts her senses and thinks the sun might indeed be the moon. But it may be a more positive shift in perception. The whole party is stuck where they are until Katherina agrees with Petruccio. Even Hortensio, who has been consistently rude to her, is asking her almost politely to do it. Katherina has often had chances to say no (sometimes with good reason) – but this time she can improve a situation by saying 'yes'.

### Or play?

When Katherina does give in, she does not do so passively. She shows Petruccio that she understands that he is going to be perverse and inconsistent – or perhaps even change his word game altogether and call the sun a candle. Whatever he decrees 'shall be so for Katherine' (line 23), she says – deftly using the name she prefers for herself, not 'Kate'.

When Petruccio tests her further in the encounter with Vincentio, she is so eloquent in both her greeting and her apology that it goes beyond obedience. It mirrors the extravagant style her husband has used throughout the first four Acts. Is she speaking with Petruccio's voice, or is this a flash of the witty Katherina of their first meeting, mocking her husband still?

**A02**

## Study focus: What is the game?

Katherina does not sound humiliated in this scene, even though she follows Petruccio's instructions. She makes a fool of herself, but also of Vincentio. Is it being suggested that a woman must follow even the most ridiculous commands her husband makes? Hortensio's last lines can be read as a male wish-fulfilment fantasy. Or has he missed the point and overlooked the playful, even **ironic** element in Petruccio's absurd requests? The answer depends upon whether we feel Katherina has gained or lost by her submission.

**A03** KEY CONTEXT

The reference to the sun and moon was a common analogy used during this period to describe the ideal relationship that should exist between husband and wife. The moon obviously 'follows' the sun and 'mirrors' its behaviour; just as a wife should behave in a way that reflects well on her husband, as his subordinate.

**A05** KEY INTERPRETATION

It is common in modern productions for Katherina to turn to Petruccio when she claims to have been 'bedazzled with the sun' (line 47) to check whether Petruccio wants her to call it the sun or the moon.

## Revision task 3: Romantic speeches

**A02**

Write notes comparing Petruccio's flattery of Katherina's beauty in Act II (244–58) and Katherina's speech to the 'young budding virgin' Vincentio in Act IV Scene 5 (38–42). Are the speeches simply mocking their subjects, or do they do something more?

# ACT V SCENE 1

## Summary

- Katherina and Petruccio take Vincentio to his house in Padua, where he finds the Merchant in his place and Tranio dressed as his son Lucentio.
- Vincentio is nearly arrested on the orders of Baptista, but Bianca's wedding party arrives and the confusion begins to be sorted out.
- Petruccio demands a kiss from Katherina. She does not like to kiss in the street, but finally does so.

## Analysis

### The masks come off

As all the characters converge, the pace picks up ready for a comic climax. Shakespeare demands of the actors that they should move *'as fast as may be'* (line 103). This keeps the comedy fresh and ensures that, even as the real Vincentio begins to think the very worst, there is no lasting hurt.

In this scene everyone begins to discard their disguises. Tranio and Biondello hurry off to change back into their everyday servant clothes. Petruccio, too, feels able to dispose of his 'mad-brain rudesby' personality (III.2.10). On the whole, the social order is restored; Lucentio kneels respectfully to his father and authority figures Baptista and Vincentio regain the upper hand at the end of the scene when they go into the house together.

However, the young people have succeeded in choosing partners for themselves. And it is **ironic** that Lucentio, the romantic, claims that 'Love wrought these miracles' (line 114). We know that his success in wooing and wedding Bianca lies with his supposed inferiors: the lady herself, and Tranio his clever servant.

### To kiss or not to kiss?

Petruccio and Katherina are spectators here and their amusement is mutual. His request for a kiss is interesting, in that it can be played in different ways. It might be yet another example of the triumphant husband testing his wife. However, the married couple use affectionate terms when speaking to one another. Katherina is 'my sweet Kate' (line 140), and he is 'thee' and even 'love' to her, rather than the formal 'you' of the previous act. His repetition of the threat to go back home if she refuses could be seen as playful – and her reply, 'Nay, I will give thee a kiss' (line 139), sounds as if she is indulging in a bit of silliness rather than being afraid of him.

### Progress booster: Exits and entrances **A02**

You may find it helpful to look at the exits and entrances in this scene and see how many characters are kept moving at speed for maximum confusion before Katherina and Petruccio are left alone for their quiet kiss. The playwright is careful throughout to ensure that entrances and exits are arranged to change a mood or to contrast one scene strongly with another.

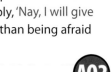

# ACT V SCENE 2

## Summary

- At Bianca's wedding feast, the other couples are rude to both Katherina and Petruccio, and Bianca leads the women out.
- The men wager as to whose wife will be the most obedient to come when called. The other two women refuse, but Katherina comes at once.
- At Petruccio's request, Katherina makes a speech about a wife's duty.

## Analysis

### The end of romance?

The scene begins with a feast, an image of harmony. We have seen Katherina's own wedding feast disrupted. Her later meals are ruined by Petruccio's apparent bad temper. Now Lucentio opens the scene by asserting, 'At last, though long, our jarring notes agree' – which is as much as to say 'and they all lived happily ever after'.

However, nobody is behaving very well. Hortensio and the Widow sneer at Katherina and Petruccio. Bianca makes a bawdy joke before flouncing out. When Petruccio remarks, 'Nothing but sit and sit, and eat and eat' (line 12), we see a flash of the old anarchic and puritanical hero of the first two acts. We might even agree with his sentiments. This bickering is, after all, not what we expect of a comedy with a happy ending.

### Gender and power

With the men left alone together, it becomes clear that the link between marriage and money is as strong as it was at the beginning of the play, when Bianca was auctioned and Katherina's dowry agreed. Men control the money, and the power. Women are objects in a game for men to win or lose. Even Baptista joins in, giving Petruccio a cash bonus, 'Another dowry to another daughter' (line 120).

Shakespeare is perhaps in the position of a scriptwriter today trying to write a James Bond film: he has to keep certain elements of the story, even if they embody views on gender half a century out of date. The awkward fit of the story of the wager with the more complex affection between the couple we saw in the previous scene can make this scene uncomfortable to watch or read.

## Study focus: Costume and meaning

**A02**

Some people consider that the commands Petruccio gives Katherina show a private understanding between them, rather than an attempt to humiliate her. He gives her an opportunity to use force against her smug sister and the sniping Widow. The order to throw down the cap is, as Bianca remarks, absurd. But in the light of the episode with the haberdasher, it holds a meaning that only the couple themselves understand. It is a chance for Katherina to show a generous spirit; it may also be Petruccio's acknowledgement that he is happy for her to abandon the shabby clothing he has forced her to wear. Tactfully, he does not order her to recite her own duties as a wife, but to instruct the two women who have been rude to both of them only moments ago.

**A04**  KEY CONNECTION

Shakespeare wrote another play in which a husband bets on his wife. In *Cymbeline*, one of his last plays, Posthumus gambles on the faithfulness of his wife Imogen. He is duped into thinking he has lost the bet and almost loses her forever.

**A05**  KEY INTERPRETATION

In many productions Katherina plays Act V Scene 2 in a splendid new dress, as if her changed personality is chiefly interested in being fashionable and 'feminine'. In Gregory Doran's 2003 production for the Royal Shakespeare Company, Alexandra Gilbreath as Katherina played it wearing the tattered remnants of the dress in which she had taken her muddy journey, Petruccio's boots and the disputed cap worn inside-out. How do you think this might affect our understanding of Katherina?

## Katherina's speech

How are we to interpret this long discussion of marriage? There are a number of contradictory readings. Some critics have argued that Katherina is not serious, and some performers have certainly chosen to deliver it with mockery. Others suggest that this is an act of love for Petruccio: she can see that, for whatever reason, he needs her to support him at this moment. Still others find the sheer length and forcefulness of the speech – the longest in the play – an indication that Katherina has found her voice.

For the first time, everyone is silent around Katherina, listening to her alone. On the other hand, some feel that she is speaking with Petruccio's voice, not for herself. Is she so cowed that she has no voice of her own? Or should we feel that, like him, she is a born performer, delighting in the use of such complex language, and that Petruccio has helped her to discover this side of herself?

## Who wins?

However we read Katherina's speech, Petruccio is the winner, with the Katherina he wants, plus a double dowry and the respect of his peers. However, as we have seen, the apparently meek women of the play reveal themselves as 'shrewish' in this scene. Perhaps his victory can only be temporary, and the fiery Katherina may return. The feeble comments of Hortensio and Lucentio suggest that there has been an overall loss of male power.

Yet it also seems that happy marriage has been shown to depend upon female submission. Petruccio's verdict, 'We three are married, but you two are sped' (line 191) suggests that his own marriage is the only one he can imagine will endure. The audience might well agree with this. Petruccio and Katherina, for all their differences, are the most original and interesting characters in the play. We do not know how the marriage will work, but it is hard to imagine them having a successful relationship with anyone else.

## Exit Katherina?

After his final speech, the stage direction reads '*Exit Petruccio*' (line 193) after his final speech, while there is no mention of Katherina. (This has puzzled some editors into altering the text in their editions.) Petruccio's earlier line 'Come Kate, we'll to bed' (line 190) may indicate that they are embracing and walk off entwined together. Or Katherina may trail off after everyone has left, resigned to her fate. Or Shakespeare might, just possibly, have arranged things so that the *Shrew* actor is left alone on the stage for a moment, to take a special bow.

## Key quotation: A kiss – not a test?

Petruccio's 'Why, there's a wench. Come on, and kiss me, Kate' (line 186) heralds the last of several kisses Katherina gives or receives in the play. This one suggests that he feels it is time to consummate the marriage.

# EXTRACT ANALYSIS: V.2.142–185

Katherina's speech is the climax of the play, almost the last word. It thus provides a closure of sorts. But it also raises questions. Petruccio has already won 'peace … and love, and quiet life, / And awful rule and right supremacy' (V.2.114–5) – and, of course, his bet. Is this a further test of obedience? Katherina only speaks here when directly told to do so. And in many ways her speech closely resembles Petruccio's. For example, she makes lists ('thy lord, thy life, thy king, thy governor' – line 143), recalling his own listing of her among his goods and chattels in Act III.

There are other links, too. The comparison that Katherina makes between an unruly woman and a muddy fountain, which no one will 'deign to sip' (line 151), links to the imagery of food, and to Petruccio's starving of Katherina during the taming scenes. She can eat now because she is a good wife – her husband's 'super-dainty Kate' (II.1.187). This may imply that her own voice is submerged by Petruccio's. However, she proves a remarkably assured user of exaggerated language and never needs to be prompted or urged on. Her description of the women's behaviour in terms of frosts and whirlwinds has the same enjoyable excess as Petruccio's macho boasts to Hortensio about lions and angry seas in Act I. We might wonder whether she is gently parodying her husband – or at least conclude that she is capable of excelling in their verbal battles.

It is worth bearing in mind, however, that the ideas expressed by Katherina in this speech are not specifically Petruccio's ideas. They come from a range of sources and essentially reflect the conservative male orthodoxy of the period. For example, the section about the 'painful labour' (line 155) of the heroic male, while the woman stays safe at home, is quoted from a book of Latin dialogues, or 'Colloquies', by the Dutch scholar Erasmus, which Shakespeare would have studied as a boy and perhaps acted out in the classroom. It is not particularly apt to the circumstances of the play, as none of the bridegrooms is ever seen to do any work.

Likewise, the idea of a woman who defies her husband as a 'foul contending rebel / And baseless traitor' (165–6) has the backing of the law: it understood a husband's relation to his wife to be exactly like the relationship of a king to his subjects. Thus a woman who killed her husband could be burned to death as a traitor to the state as well as a murderer. This detailed kind of reference would mean that an educated Elizabethan spectator might be equally interested in the manner of this speech – its learning and breadth of knowledge shows Katherina as a brilliant if conformist speaker – as in the matter of it, the harsh political reality it reflects.

 **KEY INTERPRETATION**

Charles Marowitz's successful and much-travelled 1973 adaption of the play, *The Shrew*, shows the final scene as a nightmarish 'tribunal' where Katherina is on trial. She recites her long speech in response to brutal prompts by Petruccio until she breaks down, while, on another part of the stage, a wedding is taking place.

 **KEY INTERPRETATION**

The critic Lisa Jardine points out that if obedience is meant to be a response to financial support, then Petruccio, who does not seem to do any work and has profited enormously from this marriage, should be the one to kneel to Katherina (*Still Harping on Daughters*, Harvester Press, 1983).

Although we never see a priest on stage, we frequently hear about church services in the play. The idea of the man as 'head' of the woman, and her duty to 'serve, love and obey' (line 170) is reminiscent of the English wedding service in use today. In Shakespeare's time there was a prescribed 'homily', or sermon, on that very subject, which the law required the priest to read. One such homily made Katherina's point about women's bodies: 'The woman is a weake creature, not induced with like strength and constancy of minde'.

There would also be a reading from the Bible underlining that, 'as the church is subject unto Christ, likewise the wives to their own husbands' (Ephesians Chapter 5 Verse 24). The bride took a vow to obey her husband. (This vow would remain part of the Book of Common Prayer until 1928.) Katherina is thus bringing onto the stage the words which we did *not* hear her say in Act III Scene 2. She is speaking them to the man who made a mockery of her wedding. We are told how he kissed her in a noisy and irreverent fashion. Is this now her 'real' wedding? Is the kiss Petruccio asks for now his 'real' kiss to the bride?

If this is the case, how are we to understand the final section of this speech in which Katherina offers to place her hand beneath her husband's foot? Once again, the idea is taken from the marriage service – but this time from an older form of it, no longer legal. It would have been at least forty years since any bride was expected to do such a thing. Is Katherina serious? Is she testing Petruccio's intentions? Is the playwright simply underlining her enthusiasm for marriage? Or is he harking back to what some at least of his male audience might think of as 'better days'? Petruccio does not make Katherina go through with the act; but the actor has to decide whether he responds with love, or shock, or shame.

It would have been highly unusual to hear a discussion of marriage like this delivered by a woman in a public setting. Katherina is as effective and eloquent as a minister. A speech of this length is not just a private expression of feeling. She is preaching. This was forbidden to women. Here, however, Katherina has taken the wedding sermon and the wedding vows into her own hands. Perhaps the conservatism of the sentiments is intended to reassure. It shows that a woman can dominate a gathering without undermining the social order. The Paduans are flabbergasted by Katherina's speech – and perhaps Shakespeare's audience would be too.

However, it inevitably leaves a modern audience deeply uncomfortable. The mutual spark between the couple when they are engaged in genuine dialogue suggests possibilities the speech seems to betray. It remains one of the reasons that *The Taming of the Shrew* continues to interest and infuriate audiences.

KEY INTERPRETATION  A05

In Michael Bogdanov's 1978 production for the Royal Shakespeare Company, Jonathan Pryce's Petruccio was horrified by Katherina offering her hand for him to tread on as he realised the implications for the relationship. He left with Katherina trailing after him – as Paola Dionisotti (Katherina) described it – 'two very lonely people'. Grumio remained to gather up the money Petruccio had won.

KEY INTERPRETATION A05

In an early film version of the play from 1929, Mary Pickford's Katherina gave a broad wink to Bianca as she concluded the speech, suggesting it was not to be taken seriously.

# PROGRESS CHECK

## Section One: Check your understanding

These tasks will help you to evaluate your knowledge and skills level in this particular area.

1. What tricks are played on Christopher Sly in the Induction, and why? Write a list of the tricks and suggest the Lord's possible motives.

2. What differences, if any, do you note in the behaviour of the Minola family when no outsiders are present?

3. Why do Lucentio and Tranio exchange clothes, and how do you think this affects their behaviour? Write notes outlining your viewpoint.

4. How would you describe the relationship between Petruccio and Grumio? Write notes explaining your viewpoint.

5. How would you describe the first encounter between Katherina and Petruccio? List some words that would fit a comic view, and some that would fit the reverse.

6. The last Act of a comedy often involves weddings, but here all the marriages have already taken place. Make notes on the effects this has on our view of the relationships between the couples.

7. What does Petruccio have to say to the audience on the subject of taming Katherina, and why does he think he can do it? Make brief notes on his techniques.

8. How do the other men in the play describe Katherina? List four or five examples.

9. Name some strategies the suitors use to pursue Bianca. Which do you think she finds most gratifying?

10. What financial arrangements are made around the marriages of the sisters? Make brief notes to show how these indicate each sister's relationship with her father.

11. Find three statements to show Petruccio's financial interest in Katherina. Do you think these interests are compatible with a happy marriage?

12. What are the chief differences between Katherina's journey to Petruccio's house and her return to Baptista's? Write your ideas in a two-column table.

13. Describe the experiences of Vincentio and the Merchant in the play. Who do you think has the more difficult time? Make brief notes.

14. Petruccio and Katherina both have detailed descriptions of offstage incidents involving horses. What effect does this have on their next appearance on stage? Write brief notes on each incident and its effect.

15. What tasks does Tranio have to do in order to make Bianca's marriage with Lucentio possible? Make a short list.

16. What does Hortensio learn, or not learn, from Petruccio? Write brief notes exploring the progress of their relationship.

17. List three ways Petruccio tests Katherina's obedience in the course of the play. How do their outcomes differ? Write your ideas in a two-column table.

18. What impression does Act IV give us of Petruccio's home? Write brief notes.

19. How are material objects used to create comedy? Choose six and write a sentence about each one.

20. What are the main points Katherina makes about how women should behave, in her final speech?

········································································
## Section Two: Working towards the exam
········································································

Choose one of the following five tasks which require longer, more developed answers. In each case, read the question carefully, select the key areas you need to address, and plan an essay of six to seven points. Write a first draft, giving yourself an hour to do so. Make sure you include supporting evidence for each point, including quotations.

1. Explore the different functions of clothing in the play.
2. 'The sexual politics of *The Taming of the Shrew* make it impossible to enjoy as a comedy.' Do you agree?
3. What is the value of the subplot?
4. *The Taming of the Shrew* is a play within a play. How might that affect the way the audience responds to it?
5. 'The play is essentially anti-romantic.' Do you think the way it depicts the relationships between the three couples bears out this statement?

| Progress check (rate your understanding on a level of 1 – low, to 5 – high) | 1 | 2 | 3 | 4 | 5 |
| --- | --- | --- | --- | --- | --- |
| How the relationships between Katherina and Petruccio and Bianca and Lucentio develop over the course of the play | | | | | |
| The function of the servants in both plots | | | | | |
| How the Induction raises questions for the audience to consider in the main play | | | | | |
| What role money plays in the action | | | | | |
| The different kinds of pretence and role-playing in the play | | | | | |

## CHARACTERS

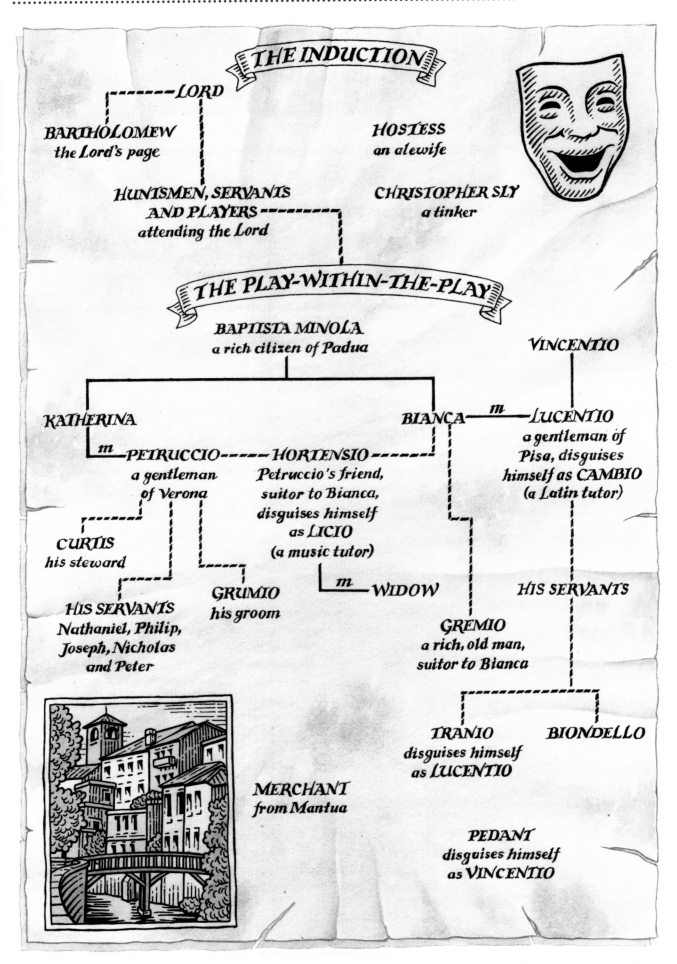

**THE INDUCTION**

LORD

BARTHOLOMEW
*the Lord's page*

HOSTESS
*an alewife*

HUNTSMEN, SERVANTS
AND PLAYERS
*attending the Lord*

CHRISTOPHER SLY
*a tinker*

**THE PLAY-WITHIN-THE-PLAY**

BAPTISTA MINOLA
*a rich citizen of Padua*

VINCENTIO

KATHERINA

*m*—PETRUCCIO----HORTENSIO-----

BIANCA—*m*—LUCENTIO
*a gentleman of
Pisa, disguises
himself as CAMBIO
(a Latin tutor)*

PETRUCCIO
*a gentleman
of Verona*

HORTENSIO
*Petruccio's friend,
suitor to Bianca,
disguises himself
as LICIO
(a music tutor)*

CURTIS
*his steward*

*m*—WIDOW

HIS SERVANTS

GRUMIO
*his groom*

GREMIO
*a rich, old man,
suitor to Bianca*

HIS SERVANTS
*Nathaniel, Philip,
Joseph, Nicholas
and Peter*

TRANIO
*disguises himself
as LUCENTIO*

BIONDELLO

MERCHANT
*from Mantua*

PEDANT
*disguises himself
as VINCENTIO*

# PETRUCCIO

## Who is Petruccio?

- Petruccio, a gentleman of Verona, is a friend of Hortensio, and has come to Padua looking for a rich wife. He is persuaded to marry Katherina.
- Once married, he takes Katherina to his house, where he bullies the servants and ensures she gets no food.
- When she finally agrees to be ruled by him, he lays a bet on her obedience.

## Study focus: A role for a star

It is easy to appreciate that Petruccio is a spectacular role for a charismatic actor. However, for anyone watching and reading the play today, there is a problem: we are enormously entertained by Petruccio, but often repelled by what he says and does. His theatricality is engaging – he is aware of himself as a performer, and clearly enjoys showing off. Sometimes his acts are **farcical** (the wedding ceremony, his behaviour with the tailor and the haberdasher) and sometimes he is the source of **slapstick** comedy. Occasionally, he bursts into song.

He is also gifted with language. His speeches in Act I Scene 2 are full of macho boastfulness, but also witty, as if he does not take himself seriously. At times his language is surprisingly poetic (like his descriptions of Katherina at their first meeting). This verbal dexterity does not necessarily make us like him, but we can enjoy the theatrical skill with which he presents himself. How exactly the audience responds to Petruccio depends on whether the actor emphasises the character's sinister and violent aspects as well as his energy and playfulness. There are elements of all these qualities in his characterisation.

**KEY INTERPRETATION** **A05**

A stage tradition of Petruccio brandishing a whip began in the eighteenth century. It features in the 1953 film of the musical adaptation *Kiss me, Kate*, where Petruccio uses it to lasso Katherina.

**KEY CONNECTION** **A01**

In 1611 John Fletcher wrote a sequel to the play, *The Tamer Tamed*, in which the gender roles are reversed. Petruccio, now a widower, marries Maria. She loves him but is determined to end his bullying ways. As Fletcher's use of the character indicates, Petruccio has always appealed to the imagination – but his conduct evidently troubled some of Shakespeare's own younger contemporaries.

### The fortune hunter

Within moments of his arrival on stage, Petruccio announces that he is seeking a wealthy wife. Taming Katherina is certainly financially rewarding. Petruccio's expenses are paid by Bianca's suitors, anxious to get Katherina out of the way. Not only does he win the wager in the final scene, but Baptista, impressed by the transformation of his daughter, offers a second dowry. The male characters generally behave as if Petruccio is performing a public service for which he deserves a fee. However, his unashamed interest in money is honest; the suitors of Bianca never really acknowledge that they are trying to buy her.

### Swagger or cunning?

Petruccio's presumption leaves Katherina and the audience dumbfounded. He storms in like a pirate to claim his bride. Although his wild clothing and strange antics at the wedding make the audience laugh, this **protagonist** is preparing us for the resolute rule he outlines to the wedding guests in Act III Scene 2 (see lines 223–40). We can never doubt that Petruccio intends to be master of what he owns, and is prepared to take on a role and work hard to achieve his aims. He is extremely single-minded, never once admitting that Katherina has her own point of view.

### Petruccio's aims

What does Petruccio really want? The ambitions he describes are quite ordinary. They are, **ironically**, at odds with the swashbuckling persona he assumes. He says that he wants domestic peace and harmony. All the noise and chaos he causes are intended to secure a quiet life at home. So how does he ensure he achieves it? Mainly by sheer will: he doggedly and persistently asserts that everything is the opposite of what it seems, leaving Katherina baffled. But also, perhaps, through play. His insistence that Katherina greets Vincentio as a sweet young girl, for instance, seems an invitation to have fun – if Katherina can suppress her instinct to say no to everything.

### Teacher or bully?

The other male characters evidently approve of his taming strategy: all are willing to assist this most masculine and dominant male. For of course, as a man, Petruccio's eccentric behaviour is socially permissible, while Katherina's is not. His **soliloquy** in Act IV suggests he sees himself as teacher and educator. His use of **imagery** from hawking implies he has skill and patience. But it also suggests his concern with his reputation as a man who can exert full control.

His behaviour implies a masculine brute force and desire to dominate. He directs a good deal of violence at his subordinates. Some of this is pretence, in which they all join, to mirror to Katherina her own disorderly behaviour. But it also reminds her what he can do, if he chooses. If Petruccio does not beat his wife, she certainly suffers physically. The neglect and insults of her father's house are replaced by deprivation: no food, no sleep, no new clothes.

### Is Petruccio happy with his success?

Petruccio does not use the word 'love' – although the word is arguably trivialised by some of the other characters. By the end of the play he is clearly satisfied with the wife he has moulded. He seems to seek kisses for their own sake, rather than using them to humiliate her, as at the wedding, or to test her. In the final scene he speaks not just of her obedience but of her 'new-built virtue' (line 124). This suggests that he values more than her willingness to follow commands. Perhaps he realises that she understands his concern to see through externals like clothes and polite manners, unlike the other new husbands and wives.

### Key quotations: Petruccio                                                    A01

When Petruccio first sees his old friend Hortensio, he says, 'I come to wive it wealthily in Padua' (I.2.74). This is an aim from which he never swerves. His final words are, 'And being a winner, God give you good night.' (V.2.193)

'Winner' sums up Petruccio, who at no point seems vulnerable. This can alienate the audience. If at any point his own happiness was at stake, the possibility of a genuine partnership within this marriage would seem more real to us.

---

**A05  KEY INTERPRETATION**

Petruccio's bizarre horse in Act III Scene 2 is an offstage accessory to his eccentric wedding outfit. It has also been interpreted as an image of his own inflated and eccentric character, or of Katherina as an exhausted animal. There is a very detailed analysis of its significance in Peter Heaney's article 'Petruchio's Horse: Equine and Household Mismanagement in *The Taming of the Shrew*', *Early Modern Literary Studies* 4.1 (May, 1998).

**A04  KEY CONNECTION**

Shakespeare's later comedy, *Much Ado About Nothing*, has sometimes been seen as an attempt to revisit and modernise *The Taming of the Shrew*. Rather than forcing a woman into conformity, the Petruccio-like hero Benedick risks his reputation and his male friendships out of love for the fiery Beatrice. He ranges himself on the side of the women against his male companions, who have condemned the innocent lady Hero for unchastity – an extraordinary action for an early modern male.

# KATHERINA

## Who is Katherina?

- Katherina is the elder daughter of the wealthy Baptista. She has a reputation as a 'shrew'.
- She is married off to Petruccio in exchange for a large dowry; he sets about taming her.
- At Bianca's wedding feast, Petruccio bets on her obedience and wins when she makes a long speech about the duties of a wife.

### 'Kate the curst'

The role of Katherina is a stereotypical one, familiar to the Elizabethan audience from folklore and **ballads**. She is the scolding, disobedient and wayward woman who must be quashed. The treatment she receives bears some resemblance to the methods used to punish 'shrewish' females: the scold's bridle and the ducking stool. Although Petruccio does not use such crude physical violence, he certainly threatens to cuff and restrain Katherina and the audience would probably expect some broad slapstick violence from them both.

## Study focus: Katherina's motivation

You should consider why Katherina acts as she does at the start of the play. Modern audiences are likely to feel that she has some cause for her distemper. Her father is cold, interested mainly in money, and makes it obvious that Bianca is his favourite. Her sister flaunts the virtues that Katherina does not possess. The Paduan males make unpleasant remarks about her. By giving her some **motivation**, Shakespeare brings originality to the old story and makes the role more complex for the actor. But he also creates problems, for the stereotype has become more human, and the audience may no longer feel comfortable at seeing her humiliated.

### Does Katherina change?

It can be argued that Katherina is stuck in her angry persona and is not capable of changing without help. Petruccio's shock treatment sets her free. It is certainly possible to track changes in Katherina's speech. At the beginning of the play she speaks in short, fiery bursts. During Act IV, her combative wit becomes more playful. Her exchanges with Petruccio about the sun and moon, and the fantasy she spins around Vincentio, suggest she is now using her wit to entertain, rather than resist, him. And her speech in Act V is eloquent and graceful. Are we to assume that she has finally found a reason for being ruled by men?

### Or is she crushed?

However, as Katherina goes from making demands to following instructions, she could be seen as becoming more and more powerless. She spends most of her time in Petruccio's house in silence; her words are either ignored or twisted. Apart from the speech in which she wonders why he shows her such 'spite' (IV.3.2), we have no insight into her thoughts. It is left to the actor to decide how to portray her reactions. Her long speech at the end of the play confirms the success of the taming by presenting a man's view of the world. Has Katherina sacrificed her own female voice? Or is she rising to the occasion with a burst of wager-winning eloquence to please her husband, with no more conviction behind it than her earlier address to the 'budding virgin' Vincentio (IV.5.38)?

### Sisterhood?

Katherina's relationship with the other female characters in the play is important. Unlike Shakespeare's other comic heroines, she has no female friend or confidante. Her isolation is complete. This, perhaps, shows us how at odds she is with society. Both before and after her taming, she shows only aggression to other women – and, to be fair, they have no kind words for her at any point. Neither her sister nor the Widow responds to her final speech. The male characters are alone when they celebrate the taming of the shrew.

## Progress booster: Love or defeat?

**A05**

As the title of the play suggests, the focus is on taming – the outcome is inevitable and the character of the 'shrew' is not especially relevant. However, the audience who enjoyed some of Shakespeare's later witty and outspoken women (such as Beatrice in *Much Ado About Nothing*) might expect to see Katherina rewarded with a loving relationship. Certainly some performers have shown Katherina in the final scene as repeating her speech robotically, terrified of the consequences of disobedience. Others lay emphasis on the fact that she does use the word 'love'. They suggest that in Petruccio she has found an ally, a fellow non-conformist.

If that is the case, her recital of all the contemporary male sentiments about marriage can be understood as her gift to him. She makes a deliberate choice not to humiliate him as Bianca humiliates Lucentio. It is also possible to assert that Katherina loves Petruccio, but with a love based in abuse: the critic Emily Detmer suggests that we can read her feelings in terms of Stockholm Syndrome – that is, the state of mind in which a victim of kidnapping or torture can fall in love with their tormentor. Shakespeare's text leaves the choice to the actor. You may find that you change your mind several times about your own interpretation of Katherina's feelings and it is a good idea to make notes on your thoughts.

**A04** **KEY CONNECTION**

In *The Tamer Tamed*, John Fletcher's sequel to *The Taming of the Shrew*, the victory of Maria, who tames Petruccio, is possible because unlike Katherina she enlists the help and co-operation of other women.

**A05** **KEY INTERPRETATION**

Emily Detmer's article on Katherina and the nature of Stockholm Syndrome, 'Civilising Subordination: Domestic Violation and *The Taming of the Shrew*' can be found in *Shakespeare Quarterly* 48, no. 3. Fall 1997.

## Key quotations: Katherina

**A01**

Katherina's first words in the play are to her father: '… is it your will / To make a stale of me among these mates?' (I.1.57–8)

Her resentment at the way her father exposes her to ridicule suggests that she is used to being betrayed by men. It is not a line the contemporary audience would necessarily expect from a traditional 'shrew' out of folk tales.

Katherina's statement after her ordeals in Petruccio's house go to the core of her character: 'I will be free / Even to the uttermost, as I please, in words' (IV.3.81–2). Words are the source of Katherina's power and personality. She is at her most wretched when she is silent. Whether we appreciate her eloquence at the end of the play will depend on whether we see her as set free to speak or forced to use the words only of her husband's choosing.

## Revision task 4: Silences

**A02**

Find three moments when Katherina remains silent. Make brief notes on the feelings an actress might be able to convey with her body, and which feelings might be impossible to show.

# BIANCA

## Who is Bianca?

- Bianca is the younger daughter of Baptista and the sister of Katherina.
- Hortensio and Lucentio court her, disguised as tutors.
- She marries Lucentio in secret and her marriage feast ends the play.

## Bianca the virtuous?

Bianca's characterisation is sketchy but intriguing. To begin with, she seems a stereotype, designed to be the polar opposite of the 'shrewish' Katherina: the quiet, obedient maiden her suitors adore. Like Katherina, she is shut up at home. She claims that she has 'never yet beheld that special face / Which I could fancy more than any other' (II.1.11–12). But even if she would like to be married she is thwarted by Baptista's policy of getting rid of Katherina first. She is her father's favourite, and shows off her obedience in order to stress the contrast to her sister.

## Study focus: Getting what you want

Think about the comparisons between main plot and subplot. If the main plot seems to insist that the scold can be brought into line, the subplot suggests the reverse. From early on there are hints that Bianca will please herself. Instead of Katherina's habit of confronting men directly, this female rebels by seeming to conform. Behind her silent and demure exterior, Bianca dupes others. She says more, and speaks more assertively, as the play progresses. Her relationships with men are conducted with great assurance. She gets on well with Tranio, the clever go-between; with the disguised tutors she uses witty and quite forceful language.

## Who is the real 'shrew'?

Bianca's submissive outward appearance gives her power: she is able to choose a husband by deceiving her father. Like most comic heroines, she marries for love. But there is a good deal of **irony** in her characterisation. Is she the real 'shrew' in this play, more dangerous than her railing, brawling sister? At the end of Act V she will not come to Lucentio, though his request is polite. She then acidly condemns him for laying a bet on her obedience. This leaves the 'happy ending' in disarray. Katherina the scold is (at least for now) silenced, but the other scold has gained what she wanted, and it seems that her reign has just begun.

## Key quotations: Bianca A01

Bianca seems to know exactly how to annoy Katherina with this reminder that she is the older sister who seems so unlikely to marry: 'So well I know my duty to my elders' (II.1.7).

She is equally assertive with her 'tutors' – the courtship will go at the pace she chooses: 'I'll not be tied to hours nor 'pointed times / But learn my lessons as I please myself' (III.1.19–20).

# BAPTISTA

## Who is Baptista?

- Baptista is a rich man from Padua with two daughters, Katherina and Bianca.
- He pays Petruccio to marry the 'shrewish' Katherina and lets two suitors bid for the hand of Bianca.
- Meanwhile, Bianca is deceiving him and she marries Lucentio in secret.

### Wealth or love?

It was quite common for fathers of the period to arrange marriages for their children with an eye to profit. However, Baptista Minola carries this to an extreme. Although he seems to care for Bianca at least, he sees both his daughters solely in terms of the market. He cleverly keeps Bianca in reserve while he follows the custom of marrying off his elder daughter first. This raises her price: as the play goes on, she is sought by yet more men. He also exploits the suitors of Bianca to find a husband for the difficult Katherina. His lack of concern for Katherina is quite blatant. He discusses her problems in public, in her presence, something that causes her great distress.

### 'The special thing'

Baptista pays lip service to the idea of romantic love. He tells Petruccio he must win 'the special thing' – the love of Katherina – 'for that is all in all' (II.1.127–8) but the topic is never mentioned again. Essentially, Baptista allows Petruccio to make off with Katherina because, as Gremio and Hortensio recognise, he wants to be rid of her. It seems just and appropriate, then, that his younger daughter gets the better of him. This is **ironic**, because Baptista puts more energy, effort and guile into disposing of his 'treasure' (II.1.32). He plays the suitors off against one another, looking for the most advantageous match. He has no objection to the possibility of the 'treasure' ending up with the elderly Gremio, who is kept in reserve in case the huge dowry falsely promised by Lucentio does not materialise.

## Study focus: A conventional role **A01**

Notice that, ultimately, Baptista is not punished for his greed. In terms of the subplot he is primarily a comic stereotype, the obstacle to true love, and according to the comic conventions he comes to accept the love-match. He may be hoodwinked by Lucentio, Tranio and Bianca, but Lucentio is, socially and financially, the kind of son-in-law Baptista might have chosen himself.

In terms of his relationship with Katherina, Baptista cuts a less attractive figure. Although he rewards Petruccio for his success in taming her, he never speaks to her once her marriage is concluded and there is no hint of reconciliation.

## Key quotation: Baptista **A01**

Baptista feels very sorry for himself when Katherina is tormenting Bianca: 'Was ever gentleman thus grieved as I?' (II.1.37)

Although Baptista largely causes his own problems, he behaves as if he is the victim of some kind of undeserved suffering because of his family.

**A04** KEY CONNECTION

Because *The Taming of the Shrew* is a comedy, Baptista's betrayal of his children is not fatal. Shakespeare's tragedy *King Lear* opens with a scene in which a father ridicules the birth of his illegitimate child and a king unjustly banishes his daughter, leading to the deaths of all of them and the collapse of the kingdom.

**A05** KEY INTERPRETATION

In her book *Shakespeare and the Nature of Women* (Macmillan, 1975), Juliet Dusinberre claims that, 'For avaricious fathers love is for women and cash is for men. When the dramatists uphold the love match against the mercenary marriage ... they uphold women's values against men's.'

# CHRISTOPHER SLY

## Who is Christopher Sly?

- Christopher Sly is a tinker (a mender of pots and pans) who is thrown out of a tavern for drunkenly breaking glasses. A Lord finds him asleep and has him dressed in fine clothes.
- When he wakes, he is told that he is a nobleman, who has been deluded for years and thinks he is a tinker.
- As a nobleman, he is entertained with a play – *The Taming of the Shrew*.

### Sly the Warwickshire man

Sly is perhaps the only truly realistic character in *The Taming of the Shrew*. Shakespeare makes him a Warwickshire man, who uses the names of real people and places in Stratford. His down-to-earth style is the opposite of the romantic and more artificial tones of the Lord, and also of the characters in the subplot.

## Study focus: Sly the mirror **A01**

Note that Sly acts as a mirror to the main characters. Like Katherina, he is transformed – although his experience is more pleasurable, and only temporary. But they share a puzzled reaction to what seems like a dream. Like Petruccio, he is bouncy, boastful and creates the same sort of chaos around him. He boasts about his ancestry (although his grasp of history is not very good), claiming that 'the Slys are no rogues. Look in the chronicles; we came in with Richard Conqueror' (Induction 1.3–4). He even fancies himself as a 'shrew'-tamer, although his efforts to subdue the Hostess of the tavern are not successful. He also shares Petruccio's unromantic approach to love, and tries to bed the 'wife' the Lord has arranged, the disguised page, with very little grace of manner.

### Sly the Chorus

Like the Chorus in the plays of Ancient Greece, Sly acts as a constant reminder that he, and we, are watching a play. Early modern theatre did not attempt to convince spectators that what they saw was real: rather, there were many references to the fact that it was an illusion.

## Key quotation: Christopher Sly **A01**

Sly gradually starts to believe that he really might be a nobleman: 'Or do I dream? Or have I dreamed till now?' (Induction 2.67)

You might think of the play he watches as a sort of dream, with characters behaving in an extreme, unreal fashion.

## Revision task 5: Unreality **A02**

Find three moments within Acts I to V which suggest a sense of dream, fantasy or play. Write short notes on each to describe the conclusion you draw about the characters as a result.

**KEY INTERPRETATION** **A05**

Bill Alexander's 1992 production for the Royal Shakespeare Company was especially preoccupied with social class. The rich Lord and his friends hired 'the Royal Shakespeare Company' to perform to Sly. There were some tensions between the actors and the aristocrats, as well as between Sly and the wealthy Lord. Sly was particularly distressed at the unfair arrest of Vincentio, and had to be reassured by the actor playing Petruccio that 'it's only a play'.

**KEY CONTEXT** **A03**

At the end of the anonymous text known as *The Taming of A Shrew*, Christopher Sly is rudely awakened, but says he has had the best dream of his whole life, and that now he knows how to tame his wife. Directors sometimes use this material to end Shakespeare's play, in order to stress the play-within-a-play structure.

# THE SUITORS

## Who are the suitors?

- LUCENTIO: A young man. He is in love with Bianca and courts her disguised as a tutor ('Cambio'). His servant Tranio impersonates him and negotiates a marriage settlement by outbidding Gremio. He elopes with Bianca and bets on her obedience at the wedding feast.
- HORTENSIO: A young man. He is in love with Bianca and courts her disguised as a tutor ('Licio'). When she prefers Lucentio, he marries a rich widow and bets on her obedience at the wedding feast.
- GREMIO: A rich old man. He is in love with Bianca and bids against 'Lucentio' (really Tranio) for her hand in marriage.

### Lucentio – a conventional lover

Lucentio is presented as a young Elizabethan gallant. We first meet him sightseeing in Padua and ripe for an adventure, full of over-ambitious plans for study. Like all would-be romantic heroes, he falls in love at first sight. Moreover, with typical enthusiasm, he does so with the first woman he sees. He does all the things expected of his role: suffering picturesquely, comparing his love to classical goddesses, praising her beauty.

Action is not his strong point. He relies on the tolerant Tranio to organise the practical aspects of wooing and wedding. He seems to have no head for money, leaving Tranio to sort out the marriage settlement, and his father to deliver the actual sum. He clearly appeals to Bianca in his disguise as 'Cambio' the tutor, but their only topic of conversation appears to be romance. It is not surprising that he discovers his wife Bianca is less sweet than he thought; he has never taken the time to know the real woman.

**A02** **KEY CONTEXT**

The name Lucentio chooses as a tutor, Cambio, means 'exchange'. This fits the idea that he is in disguise; it also reflects the importance of money in the play. In Italy, the word is still used to denote a place where currency is exchanged.

## Study focus: Lucentio – Petruccio's opposite **A02**

Lucentio's poetic language provides a comic contrast to the down-to-earth style of Petruccio. It is full of cliches, typical of Elizabethan love poems, such as 'coral lips' and breath that 'did perfume the air' (I.1.173–4). Petruccio's comparison of Katherina to a hazelnut has more originality and suggests he is actually looking at the person rather than reciting some prepared lines. Through Lucentio, the play mocks romantic convention. It suggests that falling in love and worshipping at a distance is no basis for a happy marriage.

### Hortensio – a muddled lover

Hortensio's lack of success with women makes him a source of comedy. He is rejected by Bianca, hit with Katherina's lute and let down by the Widow. Like Lucentio, he has a great deal to learn. He clearly believes in the superiority of men. His spiteful comments to Katherina suggest that he thinks his sex gives him the right to judge her behaviour. When he suspects that Bianca prefers Lucentio, he instantly thinks the worst of her. It never occurs to him that there might be something about him she does not like. He seems to think the Widow is lucky to get him.

**A02** **KEY CONTEXT**

Hortensio's assumed name as a humble music master, Licio, means 'man from Lydia'. This was a place in Asia associated in ancient history with fabulous wealth, the home of King Midas who literally turned all he touched to gold. Hortensio never joins the bidding war for Bianca, but perhaps the name is chosen to drop a hint about his true status.

Hortensio provides a link between main plot and subplot, because his one bright idea is to find a husband for Katherina, and he capitalises on the arrival of Petruccio to arrange it. Having done so, he plays no part in the bidding for the hand of Bianca. Perhaps he has no money: or perhaps Shakespeare needed the actor in another role at this point? Hortensio clearly admires Petruccio and his taming methods. By the last Act, he has handed over the task of insulting Katherina to his wife, who leads the taunting of the couple. He seems to think he is a better tamer of women than Petruccio, rashly gambling on Katherina's refusal to come when called.

## Gremio – an elderly lover

Gremio's characterisation is that of the 'Pantaloon' from the Italian **commedia dell'arte**; one of the staple plots was the courtship of a young woman by a wealthy old buffoon. Gremio adds to our understanding of the masculine values that dominate this play. He feels able to make frequent rude comments about Katherina – although he himself is the very opposite of an object of desire. This makes him a comic foil to the romantic Lucentio. His pursuit of Bianca is not very romantic, and he only really comes to life during the auction, as if money is far more appealing. To some extent he actually speeds up Lucentio's own romantic progress by helping to sort out the confusion over the identity of Vincentio and thus preventing a damaging outcome from all the disguises. At the end, he is not unhappy to have lost his love – a hearty meal does very well instead.

## Key quotations: The suitors

'I burn, I pine; I perish' (I.1.154): This line by Lucentio is exactly what a courtly lover is supposed to say, and it could be used by any of the men in this section.

'My cake is dough' (V.1.130): This is Gremio's catch-phrase, to indicate that things have turned out badly. He uses it more than once about the courtship of Bianca, and it would apply equally to the losers of the wager at the end.

# Progress booster: Understanding the suitors

The beginning of Act V Scene 2 is a useful place to review your knowledge of the suitors. Everybody enters at the beginning (except, possibly, Katherina and Petruccio, who have been watching the previous events). This enables us to observe from their speech (and body language) how they feel about the outcome of their courtship. It also sets in train the events leading up to the wager, which reveals how they think about women.

# THE SERVANTS

## Who are the servants?

- TRANIO: the personal servant of Lucentio. He pretends to be him while Lucentio is courting Bianca in disguise, and helps arrange the marriage.
- BIONDELLO: also a servant to Lucentio. While Tranio is in disguise, he pretends to be him. His main task in the play is to deliver messages.
- GRUMIO: chief servant to Petruccio. He accompanies him to Padua, and also organises all the other servants back at Petruccio's house.
- The servants in Petruccio's house who speak are CURTIS, NATHANIEL and PETER; he appears to have thirteen servants.

## Tranio – the cleverest man in the play?

Without Tranio, Lucentio would not 'achieve' (I.1.155) fair Bianca. Tranio is cleverer than his master, as most servants in the *commedia dell'arte* tradition are. He is very fond of Lucentio, and seems to have been ordered by Vincentio to keep an eye on him. Tranio appears to be well educated. He confidently advises Lucentio to read some of the more entertaining classical authors and to make sure he enjoys his education. He finds no difficulty in becoming Lucentio, easily slipping into both his clothes and his language.

According to Vincentio in Act V Scene 1, Tranio's taste in clothes is outrageously luxurious, and he is happy to boast of the wealth neither he nor Lucentio really has. Everyone accepts Tranio's disguise, even when he becomes increasingly busy as the plot thickens. At times he seems to be stage-managing the action of the subplot, especially when he sets up his master's wedding and involves the Merchant in their affairs.

## Study focus: Servants and the social order (A02)

Tranio, like all the servants in the play, is at all times serving his master's ends. Deception can be carried a long way by a clever servant – Tranio even calls for Vincentio to be arrested – but it is not punished because, essentially, it has been licensed by the role of servant. Tranio is put back in his place firmly in Act V. He is never really a threat to the social order, any more than the servants of Petruccio are – although he has certainly caused the older male characters some uncomfortable moments.

## Biondello – messenger boy

Biondello is an entertaining role to play – a cheeky page who does his best to follow Tranio's lead. He is a fast mover who bursts on to the scene with big announcements to make. Petruccio's arrival on his amazing horse gives him a moment in the spotlight, and he makes the most of it in a flurry of technical language that seems like a cue for applause. When the bridegrooms bet on their wives, it is Biondello, the lowest in the pecking order, who gets the job of summoning Bianca and the Widow. This offers a comic opportunity to the actor, and it might be funny to watch Biondello's relief when Petruccio sends Grumio to deal with the 'shrew' herself.

**A05** **KEY INTERPRETATION**

In Gregory Doran's 2003 production for the Royal Shakespeare Company, Alexandra Gilbreath addressed Katherina's line, 'Thy husband is thy lord, thy life, thy keeper' (V.2.152) directly to Bianca, who was openly gazing at Tranio. She gently took hold of her head and moved it back in Lucentio's direction.

### KEY CONTEXT A03

Beating servants is seen as comic in the Latin comedies Shakespeare knew and borrowed (their author, Plautus, was himself a slave). Many modern productions stage the occasional violence that both Petruccio and Katherina inflict on Grumio using a drum to create the sound of a blow and stress the cartoonish nature of the violence.

## Grumio – part of a double act?

Grumio is Petruccio's servant and sidekick, and comments astutely on the taming plot. He consistently stresses Petruccio's abilities to the other characters, becoming quite rude if they doubt him – notably to Gremio. He is like a licensed court jester, who tells the truth about and to his master. Grumio's early exchanges with Petruccio set up an edgy verbal combat that matches the 'courtship' of Katherina. This servant shares his master's sharp wits and ability to argue his listener into a state of exhaustion. He is capable of snappy backchat, and it seems likely that the blows Petruccio aims at him are not designed to hurt or crush him but are an aspect of their double act.

Grumio plays his part in the taming of Katherina from the outset. At the wedding he is 'caparisoned like the horse', and 'a very monster in apparel' (III.2.63–7). He may retain this eccentric outfit to dramatise Petruccio's sermons about clothes. Like Biondello, Grumio is a source of verbal comedy: his narrative of the journey home is a vivid routine for a comic performer. He also orchestrates much of the physical chaos around meals and clothing at Petruccio's house, including the taunting of Katherina with food. Grumio gets away with far more than Katherina is ever allowed to: his cheek is tolerated.

## The others – organised chaos

At least four other servants speak briefly in the scenes at Petruccio's house, but even more are named – all of them men. It looks as if Shakespeare is looking for a great burst of masculine noise and chaos to overwhelm Katherina. Grumio issues many instructions which suggest they all understand their duties and that their negligence is staged – but they stage it with relish and offer some outrageous excuses.

### KEY CONNECTION A04

The line-up of awkward servants, each with their own difficulties in getting their appointed task right, appears to be an innovation by Shakespeare. He used it again several times and similar scenes occur in many subsequent plays. Perhaps the most famous example, however, is in Oliver Goldsmith's 1773 comedy *She Stoops to Conquer*. Expecting visitors, Mr Hardcastle instructs a group of workers on his farm on how to wait at table. He warns them, 'You are not to pop out and stare and then run in again, like frightened rabbits in a warren.'

## Key quotations: The servants A01

'I am content to be Lucentio / Because so well I love Lucentio.' (I.1.215–6): Tranio explains his job and why he does it, expressed with his typical wit.

'I cannot tarry. I knew a wench married in an afternoon as she went for parsley to stuff a rabbit.' (IV.4.97–9): Biondello is a country boy, and speaks like one – and, as usual, he is in a hurry.

'Master, if I ever said 'loose-bodied gown', sew me in the skirts of it and beat me to death with a bottom of brown thread.' (IV.3.134–6): Like Katherina when she gets the measure of Petruccio, Grumio knows that the way to handle his master is through extravagant speech. Although apparently defiant, he is actually co-operating with Petruccio's plan to leave Katherina without new clothes for Bianca's wedding.

# THEMES

## Romance and marriage

### Romance: for or against?

*The Taming of the Shrew* has been described as a romantic comedy – and also as an anti-romantic comedy. It ends with weddings, as a romantic comedy should, but everyone's road to the altar is marked by tricks, lies and brute force. The contrast between the main couples is a complex one. Shakespeare seems to be using the taming plot to suggest that the kind of romance that Bianca and Lucentio enjoy could never be real. They move in an atmosphere of luxury, music and poetry. In their world the role of the man is to languish and pay clever compliments, and that of the woman is to keep him in suspense about her true feelings.

When he first sees Bianca Lucentio cries, 'thou may'st hear Minerva speak' (I.1.84). Bianca only has to say she will do her music practice to be compared to the goddess of Wisdom. The world to which Petruccio brings Katherina is one of mud, joints of mutton, and a servant with a shabby hat. However farcical some of their interactions may be, this couple is solidly rooted in a world where real marriages happen rather than love games.

### A basis for marriage

Marriage as the happy ending in Shakespeare's later plays is achieved by a mixture of romantic desire and common sense, but *The Taming of the Shrew* seems to suggest that happiness depends on female subordination, a model we find unacceptable today. However, it can be argued that Katherina's final speech does more than show the importance of female submission. She outlines the idea that men and women have duties to each another. Because he works for her 'maintenance', the woman owes her husband 'love, fair looks, and true obedience – / Too little payment for so great a debt' (V.2.154–60). It seems that both sexes have roles to play. However, Katherina's language here might make us uneasy; the word 'payment' suggests that the relationship is perhaps still unbalanced.

## Study focus: Brutal, or just realistic? **A03**

Marriage was being redefined at the end of the sixteenth century. Some early modern commentators suggested that wives should be joint governors in the household. At the same time domestic violence was legal and widespread. There were books and homilies which held that force was allowable if it was necessary for maintaining the husband's rule. Domestic violence remained a subject for comedy well into the twentieth century. The fact that Petruccio, despite the rowdy disorder he creates in the home and the marriage bed, resolves the situation without violence suggests that he is not entirely unenlightened in Renaissance terms. But he is not exactly the equivalent of an Elizabethan 'new man'. Perhaps, given that he is part of a play-within-a-play, he is characterised as just a little old-fashioned.

## Key quotation: Petruccio's expectations **A01**

Petruccio outlines his expectations for the future thus: 'Marry, peace it bodes, and love, and quiet life, / And awful rule, and right supremacy / And, to be short, what not that's sweet and happy.' (V.2.113)

Do you think that all these things can exist together in his marriage?

**A04** KEY CONNECTION

In two of his love sonnets, Shakespeare seems to sum up the approaches of Lucentio and Petruccio. Number 99 extravagantly compares his love's breath to violets and her hand to a lily. Number 130 begins 'My mistress' eyes are nothing like the sun' and goes on to describe a dark woman (like Katherina) with no special beauty, but one he values as highly as any woman written about in sentimental terms.

**A04** KEY CONNECTION

At the end of another early comedy by Shakespeare, *Love's Labour's Lost*, the women refuse to consider a serious relationship with the idealistic and romantic men until each man has spent a whole year doing something useful. *The Taming of the Shrew* is sometimes identified with a lost play by Shakespeare called *Love's Labours Won*. If this was once an alternative title, it suggests that Petruccio's resolute lack of romance and poetry is no bar to real love.

## Money and society

### Marriage and money

In this play, fathers and wooers think of marriage mainly in terms of money. Baptista sees himself as playing 'a merchant's part' (II.1.330). **Ironically**, he disposes of his greatest asset, pretty Bianca, for a fiction. As the son of a rich gentleman, Lucentio is a good catch. But it is not likely that Vincentio will offer Baptista the incredible wealth and treasure dreamed up by the wily Tranio during the auction of Bianca.

Katherina, on the other hand, proves very profitable for Petruccio. He initially intends, as he frankly puts it, to 'wive it wealthily' for twenty thousand crowns (I.2.74), a fee for taking her off Baptista's hands. But as Katherina changes she increases in value. Her dowry is finally doubled and he wins a further hundred crowns betting on her. This all goes to Petruccio as a tribute to his taming skills, but it is Katherina who earns it. She may be Petruccio's property, but she has shed the stigma of being an unwanted object carted away for cash.

### Social hierarchy

From the Induction onwards, a clear social pecking order is established. The Lord toys with his social inferior Sly for amusement. His servants obey him absolutely. The servants who take on the identities of their masters or superiors, Tranio and Biondello, go back to their roles in the end. It is likely Bartholomew the page and Sly will do so also, although the play as we have it does not tell us. Although they give orders to the servants, the women are also confined within their roles in the hierarchy. The important decisions about their future, such as marriage, are made in their absence.

## Study focus: Status and male bonding

It is clear in the play that this is a middle-class society hungry for money, goods and social position. And it is men who decide how all these things are to be valued. Luxury possessions, and the leisure to enjoy them, are all signs of social status. Boots, clothes, books, musical instruments, dogs, horses and hawks all show off a man's worth to other men. In the world of the play, women are symbols of men's power, or lack of it: Baptista has one marriageable daughter and a 'shrew', worthless until she is tamed; Hortensio and Gremio are laughable because they fail to 'achieve' the woman of their dreams; Petruccio's obedient Kate increases his prestige.

The many references to betting and cards suggest that male competitiveness and bonding are closely linked. There are male 'double acts' throughout the play, where men are seen both supporting each other and competing: Petruccio and Grumio's crosstalk; Petruccio and Hortensio joining forces to harrass Katherina at Petruccio's house; the pretended tutors 'Licio' and 'Cambio' jostling for Bianca's attention.

## Key quotation: Petruccio bets on Kate

'Twenty crowns! / I'll venture so much of my hawk or hound, / But twenty times so much upon my wife.' (V.2.73–5)

Into these lines spoken by Petruccio, Shakespeare packs a game, praise of Katherina, macho one-upmanship, and an image of women as luxury sporting goods.

### KEY CONTEXT · A03

Lawrence Stone's book *The Family, Sex and Marriage in England 1500–1800* (1977) is an excellent source of information about family relationships in the sixteenth century. It gives a useful basis on which to judge the kind of demands Petruccio is making on Katherina.

### KEY CONTEXT · A03

In *A Godly Forme of Household Government* (1598), John Dod and Robert Cleaver wrote: 'the wife ought ... to labour to bee in favour and grace with her husband. So likewise the husband ought to feare to be in disgrace and disliking with his wife.' This is a rare early modern expression of the idea that a husband ought to desire his wife's approval for his conduct as well as feeling entitled to judge hers. It is interesting to wonder what Petruccio would think about this idea after gambling on Katherina.

# Deception

## Staging the story

In *The Taming of the Shrew*, deception, illusion and transformation are woven seamlessly together. In the Induction the audience watches the Lord using both illusion and reality to convince a poor man of the fiction he has created. He uses concrete items – pictures, music, food, clothes – to persuade the tinker that he is a lord. He also employs actors to help keep up the deception by creating another illusion, the main play. The frame serves as a reminder that nothing we are watching is 'real'.

We can speculate on what happens beyond the confines of the story. We might presume that Sly will come down to earth with a bump when the Lord gets bored with acting out his fantasy. We might think that Petruccio's taming of his wife is just another temporary 'wonder' (V.2.195) or decide that Katherina's submission is utterly heartfelt. The Induction might encourage us to remember that this is an old story, about a time when people behaved quite differently. All of this is work for our imaginations to do.

## Study focus: Disguise as deception

**A02**

Disguise in the play is both a way for characters to get what they want and a way to explore a different sort of identity. Tranio sets up a hoax just as elaborate as the Lord's in order that Lucentio may court Bianca. In the process, Tranio is able to enjoy smart clothes and authority. Lucentio plays the roles Tranio encourages him to play: tutor and courtly lover. But he also presents himself as a bold and dangerous adventurer, deceiving Biondello with the story that he has 'killed a man' (I.1.230). He would clearly like to be a Petruccio. As is frequently the case in the play, it is ironic that the deceiver is deceived. Lucentio finds himself mistaken about Bianca's sweet nature.

## Disguise and identity

Petruccio uses disguise rather differently from the others. He casts himself in the role of eccentric wife-tamer, to create a new reality for himself as a married man. Like the Lord, he uses clothes, material goods and other performers – his servants – to eke out his own acting powers. What he wants is to create a lasting, not a temporary, transformation in Katherina. But although his persona is a fiction, his motives are not. He never tries to deceive anybody, least of all Katherina, about his intentions. It is ironic that the one character whose behaviour is considered odd is proved to have been telling the truth all along. Is Katherina also being deceptive in her final speech? Certainly she is performing and using words written by others. Is she playing a role for Petruccio's approval? Trying out a new identity? Or has she lost her sense of who she is?

**A02** **KEY CONTEXT**

One of the most famous speeches in Shakespeare's work states that, 'All the world's a stage' (*As You Like It*). This was a very common image of the period. The theatre was a place that showed actors taking on and discarding roles, just as in society people played, or rebelled against, their allotted social roles. The theatre was a place of illusion, but also a place to uncover the realities behind political masks and social conventions.

**A01** **PROGRESS BOOSTER**

Which characters in the play do not adopt disguises? Are some of them deceivers in other ways? Make sure you have considered all aspects of the theme of deception.

# Madness

## Sly sets the tone

The main plot is set in a framework about 'madness'. Sly is told that he has suffered a 'strange lunacy' (Induction 2.27). But he suspects a trap: 'What, would you make me mad?' (Induction 2.16) – and of course he is right. Sly is a brawling drunk, but he is never mentally unstable. He is simply fooled by an elaborate trick and does his best to deal with the world in which he finds himself. There are many references to 'madness' in this play, but it is worth reading them in the light of Sly's experience.

## Study focus: Women and madness

**A02**

In the first scene in which she appears, disobedient Katherina is labelled 'stark mad' by Tranio (I.1.69). She is certainly a sad figure: ignored, scorned and isolated by all the other characters. Her behaviour is understandable and we may well think Gremio and Hortensio deserve to be treated with the contempt they show her.

Her 'madness' clearly means her refusal to fit into the society she lives in. At the time, many women who resisted their social roles could find themselves judged as mad. Medical authorities of the day believed that possessing a womb made women especially vulnerable to insanity. The treatment of so-called lunatics was horrific, and involved beating, cold baths, bleeding and purging. Katherina would be at real risk if the 'mad' label were to be taken too seriously by her father.

## Petruccio the 'madman'?

Interestingly, Petruccio never uses the word 'mad' about Katherina. But he is labelled unstable himself. The violence, or mock violence, between Petruccio and Grumio is described in terms of madness. As Petruccio wrings his servant by the ear, Grumio boldly exclaims, 'My master is mad' (I.2.18) and Katherina's own description of him is 'half lunatic / A madcap ruffian' (II.1.290–1) and 'a mad-brain rudesby' (III.2.10). Early modern society permitted some physical abuse towards women and servants. Katherina and Grumio offer a minority verdict about the nature of madness here.

## Causing alarm

However, while this violence is tolerated in Petruccio, some of his actions do cause alarm. When he rolls into town on his horribly diseased horse, wearing odd boots and stockings and his crazy hat, Baptista cries, 'Fie, doff this habit, shame to your estate, / An eyesore to our solemn festival' (III.2.99–100). Baptista's words betray what we might today call 'status anxiety'. He doesn't want to be humiliated in public by a son-in-law who looks like a vagabond and behaves in an outrageous manner. The foolish patriarch is comic here. The idea that his wildcat daughter and a 'madcap ruffian' could be expected to behave with decorum at their wedding is absurd. The audience would be disappointed if Katherina and Petruccio became models of sobriety.

But does Petruccio go too far? His offstage behaviour at the wedding ceremony, swearing, drinking the bridal wine and throwing 'the sops all in the sexton's face' (III.2.172) is outlandish by any standards. Even if the madness is an act, Petruccio's performance can seem self-indulgent, or at least not fully under his control.

---

**KEY CONTEXT** **A03**

In medieval and Renaissance times it was commonly held that those suffering from mental illness were possessed by evil spirits, which could be driven out by beating, immersion in freezing water and periods in isolation. In the earlier part of the sixteenth century, Sir Thomas More was as much in favour of thrashing those believed to be insane to bring them to their senses as he was of flogging heretics.

---

**KEY CONNECTION** **A04**

The idea of treating inconvenient women as mentally disturbed was common long after Shakespeare wrote *The Taming of the Shrew*, and remained a powerful topic in the theatre. The central character of Tennessee Williams's 1947 play *A Streetcar Named Desire*, Blanche, is finally put in an asylum – arguably because her rape by her brother-in-law needs to be swept under the carpet rather than because she is a danger to others.

## 'Mad' together?

Why are Kate and Petruccio both presented as 'mad'? Perhaps their shouts, threats and swaggering suggest they are well matched, that each has found the partner who fulfils their needs. Petruccio's 'madness' becomes the driving force in the play, and it apparently leads to harmony. In Act IV Scene 5, Katherina accepts her husband's wilful craziness; she copies it in style when she embraces Vincentio on the road to Padua and calls him a 'Young budding virgin, fair, and fresh, and sweet' (line 38). Petruccio seems to chide her: 'Why, how now, Kate, I hope thou art not mad' (line 43).

We are now watching a different kind of 'madness'. Angry resistance to social norms has been replaced by language games. Vincentio is not offended and calls Kate 'my merry mistress' (line 54): this suggests that the combative pair are ready to take their place in society as a happily married couple. At this moment, we can view 'mad' Petruccio as a jester, a witty figure who establishes an atmosphere of carnival and misrule.

### Is Petruccio dangerous?

Act V is more ambivalent about Petruccio. He seems to relish quarrels. He and Hortensio cheer on their wives in a contest of abuse. His spotlight-grabbing exit is shamelessly egotistical – ''Twas I won the wager' (V.2.192). This suggests that, regardless of any feelings he may have for Katherina, he has not changed. In Shakespeare's tragedy *King Lear*, madness leads to enlightenment. In this **comedy**, it is only the female who needs to learn, not her unruly master.

**A05** KEY INTERPRETATION

In a 1939 production at Stratford-upon-Avon, Christopher Sly was kept on stage. He was given Tranio's line: 'That wench is stark mad or wonderful froward' (I.1.69). Even he apparently felt able to pass judgement on Katherina.

## Key quotations: Madness  **A01**

'Am I not Christopher Sly, old Sly's son of Burton Heath, by birth a pedlar, by education a cardmaker, by transmutation a bear-herd and now by present profession a tinker?' (Induction 2.16–19): Sly knows exactly who he is. He thinks the Lord is trying to drive him out of his wits and he hangs on to his identity with determination.

'That being mad herself, she's madly mated.' (III.2.245): Bianca sees both Katherina and Petruccio as unstable and seems to take a smug pleasure in the idea.

'she, poor soul / Knows not which way to stand, to look, to speak / And sits as one new risen from a dream' (IV.1.173–5): Katherina's experience in Petruccio's house is disorientating in the extreme and Curtis suggests here that she is losing touch with reality.

## Revision task 6: Madness  **A02**

Is 'madness' in the play a failure to fit the social conventions? Make brief notes on some aspects of Katherina's, or Petruccio's, conduct that critique the world they live in.

**A05** KEY INTERPRETATION

Simon Scardifield played Katherina in Ed Hall's 2006 production with the Propeller company. For him, Katherina's identity was unformed at the start of the play. He said, 'She strikes me as the kind of girl who hasn't grown into herself yet. Her looks haven't quite come together, maybe, she doesn't have a good sense of who she is; she doesn't understand the reactions she provokes in other people … she feels humiliated by her dad.'

# Education

## Who learns what?

The play is filled with references to education. They put Petruccio's wife-taming methods into a context which suggests we should view him in a favourable light, as a teacher guiding a difficult pupil. But it is not just Katherina who is educated; other characters learn in the course of the play.

When he arrives in Padua, Lucentio has come to 'institute / A course of learning and ingenious studies' (I.1.8–9). This is what, as a young gentleman, he is meant to do with his time. However, at the sight of Bianca he throws off all thoughts of 'sweet philosophy' (I.1.28). Lucentio then uses education as a romantic strategy – but he is the one in need of teaching.

He needs the assistance of the practical Tranio to win his lady. He also fails to learn much about her. His choice of Ovid's cynical *The Art of Loving* as the set text for their Latin lessons, is not very appropriate. As Barbara Hodgdon notes in the Arden edition, Bianca is better at Latin than Lucentio.

Hortensio likewise takes on the role of music master, but fails to learn how to please Bianca and never manages to play a tune. Baptista cares about the education of his favourite daughter; her accomplishments prove it. Katherina breaks lutes and never speaks Latin. But at the end of the play, she has mastered the more masculine art of rhetoric, or public speaking.

## Educating Katherina

Petruccio's approach is down to earth. He sees himself as having a natural talent. When Katherina sarcastically asks, 'Where did you study all this goodly speech?' he puts it down to his 'mother-wit' (II.1.264–5). His experience of the world, not the university, will help him. The hero has 'heard great ordnance in the field, / And heaven's artillery thunder in the skies' (I.2.202–3). Despite the doubts of the other men, Petruccio teaches his wife an orthodox moral lesson of the time: that peace and harmony in marriage depend upon wifely submission. Hortensio announces that Petruccio has 'taught' him to be 'untoward' if his Widow 'be froward' (IV.5.79–80). Baptista is delighted with the education of Katherina. He is then totally silenced by the long speech in which she teaches her sister and the Widow.

## Key quotations: Education (A01)

'I am no breeching scholar in the schools' (III.1.18): Bianca does not think much of the tuition she is receiving and will be educated on her terms.

'Petruccio is the master / That teacheth tricks eleven and twenty long / To tame a shrew' (IV.2.57–9): Tranio is the one who starts the idea of Petruccio's 'taming school' (line 55); is he trying to ingratiate himself with Bianca through this rather sinister account of what is happening to Katherina?

# PROGRESS CHECK

## Section One: Check your understanding

These short tasks will help you to evaluate your knowledge and skills level in this particular area. Write brief notes in response to questions 1 to 8.

1. Who in the main plot do you think shares character traits with Christopher Sly?
2. What does Petruccio say about himself? Should we take it seriously?
3. What do the other characters think of his methods of taming Katherina?
4. 'Madness' is a recurring theme in the play. Find three instances of the word and make notes exploring the different senses in which it is used.
5. Money and material goods are indicators of how Katherina and Bianca are valued in their society. Make a table for each of them showing what they are considered to be worth – and what they cost the men in their lives.
6. Education is a theme in both the plot and the subplot. What are the differences in the 'lessons' taught?
7. Money shows how a man fits in his society – usually through the way he spends it. Choose five items mentioned in the text which indicate a man's social position, and arrange them in order of prestige.
8. Find three instances of deception and explain how it is achieved.
9. What are the characteristics of a good servant? Do any of the servants in the play fit the bill?
10. The subplot is full of romantic lovers: what are the rules that shape their courtship?

## Section Two: Working towards the exam

Choose one of the following three tasks which require longer, more developed answers.

1. Suggest the reasons why Hortensio and Gremio fail to get the women they want.
2. *The Taming of the Shrew* hints at the future lives of three married couples. Based on your understanding of the characters, say what you think these marriages will be like.
3. 'Being mad herself, she's madly mated' (III.2.245). Explore the theme of 'madness' in the play in relation to men and women.

**A01 PROGRESS BOOSTER**

For each Section Two task, read the question carefully, select the key areas you need to address, and plan an essay of six to seven points. Write a first draft, giving yourself an hour to do so. Make sure you include supporting evidence for each point, including quotations.

| Progress check (rate your understanding on a level of 1 – low, to 5 – high) | 1 | 2 | 3 | 4 | 5 |
| --- | --- | --- | --- | --- | --- |
| How the term 'madness' is used in different ways, and the implications of this | | | | | |
| How feelings are expressed or disguised during courtship – and the consequences of deception | | | | | |
| How male characters interact with one another to keep women in check | | | | | |
| How we see different sides of the characters when they are in mixed company | | | | | |
| The part played by learning and teaching in the different strands of the plot | | | | | |
| The role of money in the play | | | | | |

## GENRE

### Comedy

In the Induction, Christopher Sly is told he is going to see a comedy. He doesn't know what this means. This allowed Shakespeare's audience, who had paid to see a 'comedy', to feel superior. But what, exactly, were they expecting?

### Heading for happiness?

The simplest definition of a comedy is simply 'a story with a happy ending'. In drama, that can often mean marriage. Shakespeare's contemporary Thomas Heywood noted, 'Comedies begin in trouble and end in peace.' But, of course, how you define a 'happy ending' will vary from person to person and society to society. In *The Taming of the Shrew* some characters get what they think they want – but Shakespeare suggests not everybody is going to live happily ever after.

### Classical comedy – a moral lesson

Some thinkers of the time talked about comedy in terms of Aristotle's *Poetics*, which were lectures written in Athens in about 335 BCE. For Aristotle, comedy represents ordinary, unheroic people. It shows people coming to grief through their own folly and it offers a moral lesson. Some audiences might apply this to Katherina. Her tendency to lash out is a flaw – but there is a reason for it, and at times her suffering seems unfair. Mixing laughter with darker emotions was disapproved of by scholars – in 1580 Philip Sidney wrote haughtily about 'mongrel tragi-comedy' – but for Shakespeare and his fellow professionals the ability to move the audience from laughter to grief and back again was part of their magic.

### Shakespeare's comic models: *commedia*, farce and festive comedies

Shakespeare knew the Latin comedies of Plautus from his schooldays. He might also have seen a **commedia dell'arte** troupe present improvised versions of these plays, using their **stock characters** and situations: stories of young lovers, overcoming the opposition of a crusty old father who wants his daughter to marry a rich old man, aided by a clever servant and, perhaps, the servant's dimmer sidekick (known as a *zanni,* from which our word 'zany' derives). Bianca, Lucentio, Baptista, Gremio, Tranio and Biondello fit these types.

The physical comedy of *The Taming of the Shrew* links it to **farce** rather than formal drama. The term literally means 'stuffing' because farce was originally designed to provide an interlude within religious plays. Farce dealt in unlikely stories, using slapstick, jokes and cross-talk. Characterisation was very basic, keeping the sort of beatings and ear-wringings endured by figures like Grumio on a comic level.

Shakespeare's comedies share aspects of the holiday festivities that punctuated life in pre-Reformation times. May Day, Twelfth Night, Shrove Tuesday and other holy days involved games, feasts and entertainments, a break not just from work but from the rigidity of the social order. Often it would be turned topsy-turvy, with authority displaced and the underdogs allowed to rule – although not for long. Sly expects 'a Christmas gambol or a tumbling trick' (Induction 2.134) and, at times, he seems to know that he is a part of one.

**KEY CONTEXT** **A03**

Thomas Heywood (c.1574–1641), playwright and actor, claimed that the theatre could teach moral lessons and drive away melancholy. The theatre was able to 'refresh such weary spirits as are tired with labour, or study, to moderate the cares and heaviness of the mind'. The Lord's servants have the same idea in mind when they offer Sly a comedy to entertain him.

**KEY CONTEXT** **A03**

The Renaissance Church disapproved of the theatre, especially comedy. An English–Italian phrase book of 1578 includes this little dialogue as a typical snatch of English conversation:

'Do comedies like you well?

Yes, sir, on holy days.

They please me also well, but the preachers will not allow them.'

# STRUCTURE

## A complex mixture

An Italian-style comedy of deception and a farcical folk tale about a man who tames his wife: the stories of Katherina and Bianca combine two comic genres as different as, say, a *Family Guy* cartoon and a TV sitcom from the 1950s. The playwright shows – even flaunts – skill in drawing them together. The most obvious way he does this is by linking the characters. The heroine of Gascoigne's *Supposes,* the source for the Bianca plot, has a husband, and no sister. Making Katherina and Bianca sisters on the verge of marriage ensures that we constantly compare their experiences of men, the marriage market, and relations between the sexes.

Shakespeare also uses other characters to interlock the stories: Hortensio and Vincentio are involved in both strands.

### Study focus: The shape of the story

**A02**

Note that the structure of the play is one used in many comedies. The first two Acts, the **exposition**, introduce a problem: the sisters are stuck at home by Baptista's stubborn insistence on their marrying in order of age. Then the people who will change this situation, Lucentio, Tranio and Petruccio, enter the scene. The main characters converge in Act III for the bustling chaos of Katherina's wedding. This is a comic **climax**, full of energy. But it at once creates questions to keep us in suspense. Will Petruccio's taming process work? Will the disguises help Bianca and Lucentio to a real marriage, or will her only chance of happiness be pretending to 'bride it' at the feast (III.2.252)?

The action moves between the two plots until everyone – even minor characters – unites for Bianca's own wedding feast in the last scene. This use of a major social ritual for a second time in the play helps make us aware of changes, which the unfolding of Act IV has hinted at throughout. The romantic plot, the artificial Italian comedy of Bianca, has taken a bitter turn. Meanwhile the taming plot, which started in abuse, moves towards **resolution**, or at least opens up possibilities in the relationship between Katherina and Petruccio. The feast brings these contrasts into the open.

**A03** **KEY CONTEXT**

A Christmas celebration, like the one envisaged by Sly, might involve electing a 'Lord of Misrule' who imposed ridiculous tasks on the most important people in the community. In the Middle Ages, choirboys would be temporarily made 'Bishops' on December 26 and could wreak havoc in the church for just one day.

### Petruccio dominates the structure

The play is driven by the star role, Petruccio, even in his absence, as other characters discuss his progress: from Katherina's speculations on his sanity to Hortensio's hero-worship. The only character with **soliloquies**, Petruccio dominates the stage while he explains himself. In each phase of the taming plot, a pattern is repeated. Petruccio decides what he wants to do and then does it. He wants to woo Katherina; he does. He decides he will marry her; he does. He decides to cut short his wedding feast; he does. At home, he also follows a pattern: first taming rebellion, then teaching a new sort of behaviour, and finally testing Katherina's conformity.

**A05** **KEY INTERPRETATION**

You can find the idea of Petruccio's three-part teaching method outlined in detail in the Preface to Brian Morris's Arden Edition of *The Taming of the Shrew* published in 1981.

## Revision task 7: Two weddings

**A02**

There are two big social rituals in the play. Make notes on:
- How each one is used for a different dramatic purpose
- What we learn about the major characters at each wedding

**A01**

## Progress booster: Commenting on structure

To improve your grade when discussing the structure of the play, be prepared to discuss how scenes are juxtaposed and the way this can change our view of the action. For instance, you might say: 'As Bianca exits in triumph to head the bridal feast, Grumio enters to describe Katherina's painful journey to her new home.'

**KEY CONTEXT** **A03**

Michael Hattaway's *Elizabethan Popular Theatre* shows that in many of the plays ordered to be played before James I at court, slapstick routines from popular theatre were a vital component. He cites the following stage direction from *Mucedorus*, involving falls, getting wet and a somersault:

'... he drinketh over her head and casts down the pot; she stumbleth at it; then they fall together by the ears.'

As he notes, this is the kind of 'Christmas gambol' Sly has in mind (Induction 2.134) and which he enacts in his relations with the Hostess.

## The Induction framework

Framing the romantic plots within the Induction means that, right from the start, the audience is made to think about performance. Sly is a realistic character from rural Warwickshire. But from the moment he falls down drunk, everyone he meets is involved in tricks, deception and, in the case of the players, the professional theatre.

The Induction **foreshadows** aspects of the main plot: the part played by food and clothing; the running **metaphors** about hawking and hunting; the use of social power and control. These links invite the audience to question what they see and draw comparisons between the Lord and Petruccio, Katherina and Sly. But even without these parallels, the presence of Sly and his 'wife,' the disguised boy, make it hard to forget we are watching a piece of art, not real life.

Using the device of a play-within-a-play gave the playwright a chance to evoke older theatrical styles, sometimes with nostalgia and sometimes for laughs. Arguably, the main action of *The Taming of the Shrew* mocks the styles in which it is written. The complications of the ***commedia dell'arte*** Bianca plot suggest that there is no time for the lovers – or the writer – to consider what 'being in love' actually means. The taming story is not a straightforward farce. When Katherina says that her heart – rather than her self-will – will 'break' (IV.3.80), she undercuts the laughter. Penny Gay suggests in *The Cambridge Introduction to Shakespeare's Comedies* that in the Induction we see Shakespeare probing the limits of these old forms, especially their neatly resolved endings.

The Induction framework challenges the audience to relate old clichés to their lived experience. Seeing 'Bartholomew the page' dealing with his unfamiliar dress reminds us that Katherina and Bianca are not 'real' women. They are boy players who will not have to live out the consequences of the marriages in the story. Petruccio's speeches about storms and lions resemble those of Marlowe's epic heroes, Tamburlaine and Faustus. They underline the fact that within the Induction framework he is the star actor of a troupe of players – and the fact that his heroics are about taming an angry young woman makes him slightly absurd. Whether they find the ending of the play satisfactory or troubling, the audience has not been allowed to take gender relationships entirely for granted.

**KEY INTERPRETATION** **A05**

In 1963, the innovative Nigerian company Travelling Theatre took the ideas about theatricality in the Induction to an extreme. Like the Lord, they played a practical joke. The audience was told that the cast had not turned up and that they would have to perform the play themselves. Although actors were planted in the audience to take on the major roles, the audience was constantly involved and invited to debate the 'battle of the sexes' as the play progressed.

# LANGUAGE

## Blank verse

The play is a mixture of prose and **blank verse** – unrhymed **iambic pentameter**. This verse form closely resembles natural speech and Shakespeare uses it very flexibly. At times it calls attention to itself. The speaker utters a substantial piece of poetry, rather as a character in a musical performs a big number. The effect is to make the audience take notice, perhaps even applaud. An example is Petruccio's speech about his heroic past: 'Have I not heard great ordnance in the field, / And heaven's artillery thunder in the skies?' (I.2.203–4). The iambic rhythm is very powerful, five strong beats to a line like a drum, and the words are not those of everyday conversation.

Similarly, Lucentio's speech is formal as he adores Bianca from afar: 'O yes, I saw sweet beauty in her face, / Such as the daughter of Agenor had' (I.1.166–7). The five-beat rhythm is again very clear – the verse is measured, so that it resembles a song. The speech is packed with allusions to classical mythology, as if Lucentio lacks the confidence to talk about his own feelings and has to do it through books.

## Sharing verse

However, at other times the verse is unobtrusive. If you listen, rather than looking at it on the page, you may not be aware that the characters are speaking verse at all. But there are moments when it can have a remarkable effect. When Katherina and Petruccio first meet, for instance, they slip into iambic pentameter (II.1.211–3):

KATHERINA: If I be waspish, best beware my sting.

PETRUCCIO: My remedy is then to pluck it out.

KATHERINA: Ay, if the fool could find it where it lies.

On the surface this is banter. But the fact that they are copying each other's rhythm exactly suggests a strong relationship is developing, even if they are not aware of it.

## Verse, prose and social codes

Traditionally verse in drama belonged to the upper classes; servants and the lower characters used prose. Biondello, Sly and Petruccio's servants use prose to great effect. It is these characters who place the story in a very solid world. Even in a daze, Sly can talk about the inns around Stratford and his debts – 'fourteen pence on the score for sheer ale' (Induction 2.32). While Petruccio rants at the tailor to shock Katherina, the tailor himself and Grumio swap technical terms like 'trunk sleeve' and 'small-compassed cape' (IV.3.138–40). They remind us that the pride of a craftsman (and his living) are at stake, as well as Petruccio's taming programme. Some characters also make transitions between prose and verse; Sly sometimes finds himself speaking verse as a 'Lord'.

Perhaps this strange new style of speech surprises Sly himself. He certainly has to check with the real Lord to find out the correct way to address his wellborn 'wife'. His experiments with speaking verse allow the actor to create comedy by making a **metatheatrical** joke for the audience.

Tranio is an unusual servant, in that he speaks in verse as fluently as any of the well-off characters. This reflects his cleverness as stage-manager of Bianca and Lucentio's courtship. He 'becomes' Lucentio with ease. He certainly convinces Bianca's other suitors that they have cause to worry, and chats with Bianca on equal terms even though she knows his real identity.

**A02 KEY CONTEXT**

It is helpful to get the iambic rhythm into your head by marking out some lines showing the strong stresses, e.g.

'If *I* be *WASP*ish, *BEST* be*WARE* my *STING*.'

Shakespeare does not always make his lines conform so rigidly to this beat, but keeps it in the background throughout, as a jazz musician will play with a rhythm but return to the main theme at times. If a line is difficult to interpret, the rhythm can give a clue as to how it should be spoken, such as allowing Katherina to spit out the key word, 'STING', with maximum force (II.1.211).

**A03 KEY CONTEXT**

Shakespeare seems to have introduced new words and expressions to the English language, or at least to have been the first person to write them down. For instance, *The Taming of the Shrew* has the first recorded use of the word 'pedant', used by Hortensio. In Act I Scene 2 the suitors praise Petruccio for his willingness to 'break the ice' and approach Katherina, the first time this expression is known to have been used. His audience may have heard many words that were new to them. Perhaps they found this one of the pleasures of the play.

**KEY INTERPRETATION** **A05**

In 1961 the critic William Empson described the conflict between Katherina and Petruccio as one of language – making some assumptions about women and speech that seem to belong to a distant era: 'The male part of the audience may decently rejoice, not at seeing a woman beaten down by the superior strength of a man, but at seeing the offensive strength familiar in their wives overwhelmed by a man who can nag back just as unreasonably as a woman.'

# Study focus: Competitions and quarrels **A02**

In their different ways all the characters are verbally exuberant and like to compete in words. Katherina snaps at Bianca, who fights back with calculated sweetness. Gremio and Tranio-as-Lucentio make their wealth and treasure sound like something from a fairy tale as they bid for Bianca. Katherina and Petruccio, of course, argue from the moment they meet, and they do it in an impressive variety of styles. In their first scene they make use of **stichomythia** at a fast pace. Her speech is insulting, his often bawdy, but they are always capable of capping the other's line or changing the meaning of a word with lightning speed.

While Katherina is silent for much of Act IV, there comes a point when her 'discussions' with Petruccio take on a surreal wit – whether the sun is the moon, whether Vincentio is a man or a girl. Here she seems to find a way to compete with him as an equal, in terms of language at least. As they address Vincentio as a girl (Act IV Scene 5) Petruccio offers a conventional praise of 'her' beauty. 'Such war of white and red within her cheeks' (line 31) is the sort of language that Lucentio might use. Katherina goes one better. By speaking of the 'girl' as the daughter of lucky parents and a 'lovely bedfellow' (line 42) for a fortunate man, she is taking the role of a bold young suitor – not echoing her husband's opinion but offering a mild parody of a courting male. She is obeying, but also competing – and raising the bar.

## Petruccio as master of language

Petruccio dominates the play through language. He has twice as many lines as everyone else. But he is also a master of more styles; he can speak to people in the language they use themselves. So, when assuring Hortensio that he can woo Katherina, he refers to the classics like the other suitors (although he refers to women notorious for 'shrewishness' or lack of allure rather than celebrated beauties). With Baptista he talks about 'specialties' and 'covenants' (II.1.125–6), like one merchant to another.

**KEY CONTEXT** **A01**

The initial argument between Katherina and Petruccio can be seen as an example of flyting, a literary tradition that goes back centuries in England. Exchanges of insults as a form of entertainment have been enjoyed in many cultures, from the medieval court of the kings of Scotland to freestyle rap. Katherina is able to use her wit here far more creatively than she can with the suitors, who offer only very basic insults.

## Key quotation: Petruccio and comic exaggeration **A01**

Petruccio is a brilliant storyteller, clearly feeling no obligation to tell the truth . His report to Baptista about his wooing is typical : 'She hung about my neck, and kiss on kiss / She vied so fast, protesting oath on oath, / That in a twink she won me to her love' (II.1.312–4). This comic exaggeration is typical of Petruccio. He will describe things as he wants them to be, and stick to this version of reality until he gets his own way.

## Further key quotations

In his house Petruccio uses a large vocabulary of picturesque and inventive abuse, grounded in homely images his servants can understand if not appreciate. Katherina's cap is a 'custard-coffin, a bauble, a silken pie' (IV.3.85); a servant is a 'beetle-headed, flap-eared knave' (IV.1.143).

# Katherina's language

Katherina is the chief character (other than loyal sidekick Grumio), with whom Petruccio can indulge in competitive wordplay. She has far less to say than he does, and her range of reference is not nearly so wide. Her vocabulary of insults – several times she uses the stock insult 'stool'– suggests a narrower range of experience. It reminds us that Baptista keeps his daughters away from the world. But the speed of her wit matches Petruccio's, and once she has given ground at the end of Act IV, she begins to speak at greater length.

Her final speech is utterly different from the language anyone has used so far. It is formal and measured. The imagery of war and conquest implies that Petruccio has won the battle, but it is not directed at him personally. It is as if she is making a political speech, rather than giving in to an individual. It is the most carefully constructed piece of **rhetoric** in the play. The sentences are long; the grammar is complex. She presents arguments geared to her on-stage audience. She tells the sneering widow and the sister who flaunts her superior attractions that their behaviour will leave them 'bereft of beauty' (V.2.149). At the same time she offers the men some flattering images, comparing them with heads of state. The sentiments in the speech are conservative and not very congenial to us, but her control of this difficult language establishes her as a woman of intelligence who is no longer ignored in company.

**A03**  **KEY CONTEXT**

Learning for women could be risky in early modern England. In 1546 Henry VIII's last wife, Catherine Parr, expressed some of her own religious views and was in grave danger of arrest for heresy. She saved herself with a speech to the King in language very like Katherina's in Act V, telling Henry, 'Yet must I, and will I, refer my judgment in this, and in all other cases, to your majesty's wisdom, as my only anchor, supreme head and governor here in earth, next under God, to lean unto.'

**A03**  **KEY CONTEXT**

When Elizabeth I addressed her troops as they prepared for the expected invasion by the Spanish Armada in 1588, she went, like Katherina, through the motions of acknowledging some accepted wisdom about women's bodies, beginning, 'I know I have the body of a weak and feeble woman but I have the heart and stomach of a king, and a king of England too.'

## Revision task 8: Playing yourself  **A02**

Katherina and Petruccio both use language like skilled improvisers who are aware they are playing to an audience.

Make notes on how they do this in:

- A scene in which they compete with each other in language
- A scene in which they are performing to other people

**KEY CONTEXT**  **A03**

The linking of shrews and hell was traditional during the period in which the play was written. These small mole-like creatures with their large noses were commonly associated with dark, sinister forces. The 'little din' (I.2.198) that the shrew Katherina makes is intended to add to her characterisation as a scold. Shrews were thought to be noisy, aggressive and voracious little beasts.

**KEY CONTEXT**  **A03**

A woman's tongue was often seen as an instrument of the Devil. A 1557 book by the Dutch scholar Erasmus contains a story about a man who marries a dumb wife. With the help of the Devil, he gives her a tongue made from a leaf, and she begins to speak – too much, he decides, and asks the Devil to make her dumb again. But the Devil replies, 'If a woman begins once to speak, I nor all the devils in hell am able to make a woman be silent.'

# Imagery

Throughout, we find particular images developed and explored across the play rather than confined to a single remark. These help to colour our overall impression of the action, the characters and the world of the play.

## Katherina – 'fiend of hell'

Katherina's 'shrewishness' is linked to images of hell. These images demonstrate the feelings of the Paduan men towards her wayward behaviour and, especially, her sharp tongue – and establish the idea that many of the male characters are rather frightened of her. This comes across clearly in Hortensio's and Gremio's exclamations in Act I, particularly Hortensio's line, 'From all such devils, good Lord deliver us!' (line 66). Katherina is 'this fiend of hell' (line 88), fit only to 'go to the devil's dam' (line 105). Gremio wonders whether he and Hortensio will be able to find 'any man [who] is so very a fool to be married to hell' (lines 124–5). Even her father refers to her as a 'hilding of a devilish spirit' (II.1.26).

All these references establish an image of Katherina as not quite human. At one point, her actions and the men's words seem to fit together: Hortensio comes on clutching an injured head, claiming that Katherina's blow comes from a 'most impatient devilish spirit' (II.1.150). But surely the worst we can accuse Kate of is possessing a bad temper? Perhaps the accusations of 'devilry' reveal something about the Paduan men and their refusal to take any responsibility for their part in provoking Katherina.

It is significant that Petruccio disregards all the warnings he receives about uniting himself in marriage with 'hell'. After the episode with the lute he announces boldly that he loves her 'ten times more than e'er I did' (II.1.160). This may be as big an exaggeration as those glib references to the devil, but it demonstrates two things about Petruccio. First, he is not such a fool as the Paduans; he may refer to himself in heroic terms, but he knows that in marrying Katherina he is not really taking on the forces of evil. Second, he raises the idea in the audience's mind that Katherina is potentially lovable.

## Animals, hunting and hawking

The play, especially in the Induction and the main plot, uses imagery from nature. Much of the 'nature' that we see, however, is not 'natural' in the sense of untamed. It is subject to strict control. The Lord of the Induction speaks with expertise about the condition of his hounds. He also seems to control his respectful huntsmen. Is this the kind of control that Petruccio wants in his own household?

## Horses

Petruccio's use of horses adds to our impression of him as a crafty hunter. The ailing beast he rides to his wedding is clearly a part of his strategy. But is the point to humiliate Katherina, or to intrigue her? The Induction describes the ultimate in luxury mounts: 'Or wilt thou ride? Thy horses shall be trapped / Their harness studded all with gold and pearl' (Induction 2.39–40). Petruccio's horse is the very opposite of a status symbol. He might be mocking Katherina's values here – or just those of Baptista, who encourages suitors to bid for Bianca with 'six score fat oxen' (II.1.362).

On the way home Katherina's horse stumbles, 'and she under her horse … in how miry a place' (IV.1.65–7). Petruccio bullies Grumio for letting it happen, and Katherina drags herself through the mud to stop him. The taming process is under way, but, as Grumio notes, nature is hard on everyone: 'winter tames man, woman and beast, for it hath tamed my old master, and my new mistress, and myself' (IV.1.20–1).

## Study focus: Hawking

**A02**

The most developed animal imagery in the play comes from falconry. This was an expensive pursuit – not exclusive to the aristocracy, but certainly associated with it. Through it Petruccio is presented as the most 'gentlemanly' character in the play. His methods exactly match those used by a gentleman training his hawk. The hawk was kept hungry until it was willing to feed from the falconer's hand. It was also kept awake for long periods – during which the falconer too had to stay up to 'watch' his bird. Petruccio spells this out (IV.1.179–84):

My falcon now is sharp and passing empty,
And till she stoop she must not be full-gorged,
For then she never looks upon her lure.
Another way I have to man my haggard,
To make her come and know her keeper's call:
That is, to watch her …

The hawk must not control its master. On the other hand, the falconer must respect his hawk, not break its spirit. It is not a slave or a pet.

## Nature and marriage?

In the final scene much banter is associated with animals. Petruccio taunts Tranio as a failed hunter and – perhaps smarting at his status as Lucentio's 'greyhound' (line 53) – Tranio retorts ''Tis thought your deer does hold you at a bay' (V.2.57). In this scene the men seem carried away by blood-sport imagery and their bet on their wives as if they were animals perhaps springs from this.

**A04**  **KEY CONNECTION**

The best modern account of the process of taming a hawk is Helen Macdonald's *H is for Hawk* (2014), which relates how the author tamed her goshawk Mabel. The techniques are almost exactly the same as those Petruccio describes in *The Taming of the Shrew* and the relationship between the falconer and the hawk is seen as passionate, absorbing and respectful. Barry Hines's book *A Kestrel for a Knave* (1968) also provides an excellent account.

**A01**  **PROGRESS BOOSTER**

It will help your grade to show that you have a grasp of the play as a whole. Depending on the question, you might do this by discussing how a theme or image is picked up from another point in the text, or how a character seems to have changed since his/her last appearance, or how a deception is becoming harder to sustain.

### Clothing and food

Aptly for a story so occupied with the idea of marriage as a business venture, the play is filled with talk of material goods, from merchant ships and horses to lutes and dishes of tripe. Goods are a way to display wealth and they can also be given or withheld to control people.

### Clothing

Clothing is used to contrast appearance and reality. Sly is put in 'a costly suit' (Induction 1.58) and given a 'wife' (a page in a dress). This helps convince him that he is a lord. In the play attractive appearances have great power. Similarly, because Tranio wears 'a silken doublet, a velvet hose, a scarlet cloak and a copatain hat!' (V.1.59–60) he can demand that Vincentio be put in jail. Once unmasked, he is threatened with having his nose slit. However, because Vincentio is pleased with his rich daughter-in-law, Tranio's fate is merely to get back into servant's livery. He joins the servants who carry tables for the feast in the final scene.

## Study focus: Rich to poor   A02

Be aware of the importance of clothing in the play. Hortensio and Lucentio dress as poor scholars – but it is one of the **ironies** of the play that they learn nothing. Petruccio dons the most radical disguise of all. His clothes are so terrible that Tranio (in Lucentio's doublet and hose) offers to help him change. Though his clothes get a laugh, Petruccio's point is serious: 'To me she's married, not unto my clothes' (III.2.116). He clearly expects Katherina to look beyond appearances. When he abuses her new cap and gown, he is perhaps proving to her that she cares about convention more than she thought. By denying her the cap, she feels he is disrespecting her as a 'gentlewoman'. He responds, 'When you are gentle, you shall have one too, / And not till then' (IV.3.73–4). But perhaps he is doing something more. When he tells Katherina in the last scene 'that cap of your becomes you not' (V.2.127) he may be inviting her to stop imitating Bianca and conventional 'gentlewomen' and share his own anarchic disregard for appearances.

### Food

Appetite plays a major role in the play, and is linked to mental health. Petruccio sends back the burnt meat at dinner because he and Katherina are both 'choleric' – given to anger. It can lead to comedy: Grumio's taunting of Katherina with a variety of dishes may give rise to a lively chase. Hunger is also a result of disorder. While marriage should be celebrated with feasting, the two unorthodox weddings and a spoilt bridal dinner do not give anyone much nourishment. The tamed Katherina is allowed to eat at the final feast, but it is in fact a celebration for everyone, a successful social ritual. Lucentio declares that the quarrelling is over – the banquet will 'close our stomachs up / After our great good cheer' (V.2.9–10).

# PROGRESS CHECK

## Section One: Check your understanding

These tasks will help you evaluate your knowledge and skills level in this particular area.

1. What features mark the play as a comedy? What sort of comedy?
2. From what the characters say, what are the characteristics of a 'devil'? Make a brief list.
3. How does Christopher Sly respond to the food given him by the Lord's servants? What does his response tell us about him?
4. What sports feature in the play and what do they tell us about the people who play them? Write your ideas in a two-column table.
5. Which characters are the targets of slapstick comedy, and what kind of impact does their physical experience have on them? Write your ideas in a two-column table.
6. The lovers in the play use poetic language – does this reflect their true feelings?
7. The play alternates between plot and subplot to increase suspense. List some moments you might describe as 'cliffhangers' and note the questions the audience might be asking themselves.
8. Which characters use language associated with work, and why? Write your ideas in a two-column table.
9. The text suggests that Katherina and Bianca differ greatly in looks and dress, as well as in manner. Write notes on each character with this in mind.
10. The physical appearance of *commedia dell'arte* characters is often based on animals. Which characters are compared to animals, and what does it suggest about them? Write your ideas in a two-column table.

## Section Two: Working towards the exam

Choose one of the following three tasks which require longer, more developed answers.

1. Comedy is often concerned with characters who learn social lessons – or who fail to do so. Which characters in *The Taming of the Shrew* do you consider to have learned nothing at the end of the play, and why?
2. 'Shakespeare's use of food in the play is central to our understanding of some of its key themes.' To what extent do you agree with this statement?
3. How are verse and prose conventions used to express personal and social relationships?

**A01** **PROGRESS BOOSTER**

For each Section Two task, read the question carefully, select the key areas you need to address, and plan an essay of six to seven points. Write a first draft, giving yourself an hour to do so. Make sure you include supporting evidence for each point, including quotations.

| Progress check (rate your understanding on a level of 1 – low, to 5 – high) | 1 | 2 | 3 | 4 | 5 |
|---|---|---|---|---|---|
| How the playwright creates comedy by mocking the language of romantic love | | | | | |
| How clothing can reflect or hide a personality | | | | | |
| How particular images run through the play, and how they can affect our view of a character | | | | | |
| How the play is structured around repeated situations, such as feasts and other scenes where food is served | | | | | |
| How suspense is created | | | | | |

**KEY CONTEXT** **A03**

The period in English history during which Shakespeare was writing has been given several different names and it may help to bear some of these in mind. 'Renaissance' means 'rebirth', and was used to describe an upsurge of curiosity and cultural experiment that spread across Europe from the fourteenth century onwards. The term 'early modern' is used of the period from the fourteenth to the eighteenth centuries, when many ideas we now take for granted took shape. Both terms are problematic in that they give the impression that social change takes place instantly. People do not become 'modern' all at once, or shed old ideas completely.

# CONTEXTS

## Historical context

### Religious upheaval and the spoken word

When Shakespeare was a child, his father supervised the whitewashing of the Guild Chapel in Stratford, covering up the vivid mural of the Last Judgement on the walls. This experience reflects the profound changes to everyday life through the establishment of the English Protestant Church. The monarch, not the Pope, was head of this church; services were in English rather than Latin and the Bible was translated. There was a widespread rejection of images – religious paintings, stained glass, statues of the saints – that had once served to educate people in their faith. Instead there was a new emphasis on the Bible as the word of God: on words, rather than visual images, as the means of communication. The old plays performed by the citizens to show scenes from the Bible were censored.

Arguably, this cleared the ground for a professional theatre in which the spoken word would be central. Shakespeare's audience would talk of going to 'hear' rather than 'see' a play. The drama drew people deprived of colour and spectacle in the churches and encouraged them to collaborate with the actors in imagining different worlds. It engaged them with new stories: unlike the Bible plays, the endings were not already known. Without the English Reformation, Shakespeare's theatre might not have proved such a magnet for talented writers and performers. Along with other plays about acting and performance, like *A Midsummer Night's Dream*, *The Taming of the Shrew* celebrates that power. Sly is charmed with a poetically-evoked vision of a life he has never really led. Then he settles down to watch a story brand new to him, performed by professionals who open up a world of Italian intrigue and romance.

### English

The play, like much of the literature of the period, celebrates the English language. For centuries it had been assumed that, if you had something serious to say, then Latin was the language in which to say it – from philosophy and law to medicine and epic poetry. But with increased literacy, new ideas from all over Europe, and a new confidence in England's political power, English vocabulary grew. The language became a wonderfully flexible medium. In *The Taming of the Shrew* words from a whole spectrum of sources come together to enrich one another: scraps of Latin, bits of Spanish, popular songs, sporting terms, craftsmen's technical language, proverbs, snatches from the best-known plays of the day and words unique to Shakespeare's own bit of Warwickshire. Characters use different kinds of speech that reveal their social station – but everybody is highly articulate.

### Marriage and women

The Roman Catholic Church had laid great stress on the virtue of virginity. Marriage was second-best, a solution for those who could not manage total abstinence. Protestantism preferred to celebrate fidelity within marriage, the basis for a virtuous family. This new emphasis had implications for both sexes. Men and women were not considered equals; it was believed woman was made for man, who was expected to exercise 'awful rule' (V.2.115) over his wife, like Petruccio. Both, however, ruled the children and the servants. A wife might have real control over a large household if her husband trusted her. While the Church might praise 'companionate marriage', it could only happen if both parties entered into it freely. Forced marriage, for either sex, would jeopardise it. As the seventeenth century dawned, even divorce was debated, although not as a real possibility for most people.

**PROGRESS BOOSTER** **A01**

To improve your answers, show that you are aware of the historical context in a way that is clearly relevant. For example, don't write 'Shakespeare was born in 1564' but 'During Shakespeare's lifetime, the English Reformation had a profound impact on people's understanding of marriage, and this is reflected in the play's preoccupation with the importance of marriage and women's choices.'

Even this limited notion of power for women was enough to cause anxiety – especially with queens ruling both England and Scotland. Elizabeth I did not marry and become an obedient wife, but she constantly encouraged the idea that she might, showing herself both a good Protestant and an independent ruler. For every sermon or book on 'companionate marriage' and loving partnership, there was one which described women as inferior and dangerous.

The stage was a natural place on which these issues could be explored. Was true love more important than, say, a parent's desire to arrange a prosperous match? If a partner was unfaithful, what should you do? What happened if you fell in love with someone who was really unsuitable? If you read the titles of plays staged over Shakepeare's lifetime, it is surprising how many contain words such as 'Woman', 'Maid', 'Duchess', 'Queen', 'Girl', 'Wife' and, of course, 'Shrew'. The contrast between the romantic subplot of *The Taming of the Shrew,* and the struggles of Katherina to come to terms with a marriage she has not chosen, would have been profoundly interesting for the audience.

## Social welfare

Under Elizabeth I's father, Henry VIII, the monasteries had been closed down. This meant that the poorest people in the country had no place to turn. Wanderers, vagabonds and the unemployed faced terrible penalties. If a person could not prove they were attached to a 'master' and had legitimate work, they could be whipped, branded or put in the stocks. It is worth bearing this in mind when looking at the relationships between servants and masters in *The Taming of the Shrew*. It is not surprising that Christopher Sly is anxious to insist on his own identity. A tinker would need to produce a licence from two justices of the peace if challenged. The Hostess's threat of the stocks is very real. The hierarchy we glimpse in the play was, in real life, rigidly enforced. Punishments were not only violent. They were public, a demonstration of the state's power. An unfaithful husband, an unruly wife, could find themselves on the receiving end of rough justice from the community.

## Shakespeare's theatre

### The audience

Almost everybody in London, except those too poor to afford the penny entrance fee or those who considered acting to be intrinsically wicked, went to the theatre. The audience was as diverse as the cast of *The Taming of the Shrew:* lords, tinkers, craftsmen, merchants – and of course their wives and daughters. This gave companies the confidence to show a whole society to itself – how everyone was in a sense a 'player', performing their own social role, from 'obedient wife' to 'king'. The name Shakespeare's company chose for its new venue in 1599, The Globe, reflects this. The motto on their flag was *totus mundus agit histrionem* – roughly, 'Everyone's an actor.'

**A03** **KEY CONTEXT**

The best-known work about the wickedness of female rule was written in 1558 against three Catholic queens: Mary I of England, Mary of Guise, and Mary Queen of Scots and was called, *The First Blast of the Trumpet against the Monstrous Regiment* [ie. Rule] *of Women.* Its author, John Knox, was left uncomfortable when a Protestant queen, Elizabeth I, came to the throne.

**A03** **KEY CONTEXT**

Women did sometimes publicly join in the debates about gender in early modern England. One notable pamphlet was published under the name 'Jane Anger' in 1589. It explored the question of women talking too much. Jane Anger considered that men's tongues were also a problem because they were 'slippery' rather than truthful – and that men had an excessive desire to express their opinions in writing.

In Marlowe's *Doctor Faustus*, and several other plays of the period, the balcony and the pit are used to show heaven and hell. Katherina might be standing on the trapdoor to the pit while being compared to the devil, just as Hamlet would later talk about the heavens as a 'roof fretted with golden fire' while looking up at the ceiling of the theatre, which was painted with gold stars.

## The playhouse

It is impossible to show a 'world' on stage and to maintain an illusion of reality. Realistic scenery takes time to change. But the broad, bare, open stage jutting into the audience, with actors and spectators alike lit by the afternoon sun, could do just that. Instead of scenery, a few words set up a location for the audience: the Lord's luxurious mansion, Petruccio's chaotic one, Baptista's elegant Italian villa, are evoked by the ways the actors speak and behave. On this stage a balcony might be the battlements of a castle, the home of a classical god, or a handy location for musicians. Beneath the stage was a pit which might become an open grave – or hell.

## The players

The actors did not try to convince an audience that their characters were real people. It was part of the pleasure of play-going to see an actor assume his role and to collaborate with him in a shared experience – as when Petruccio demands of the audience if any shrew-tamer can do better. Renaissance plays are full of **metatheatrical** jokes, reminding the audience that they are just plays. For example, Grumio is playing an Italian character, but when someone speaks Italian he can't understand it (I.2.25–8).

A02

## Study focus: Boy players

Note that the distance between actor and role was especially marked in the case of the boys and young men who played women. Their experience was like that of modern actors playing aliens in a science fiction film. They could show their character as an individual with powerful feelings, but their main job was to convey a species. There are many generalisations about women in plays of the period spoken by female characters – like Katherina's remark that 'women are so simple' (V.2.167). Hearing them spoken by a man might have a substantial effect on the way the audience responded to them.

Richard Madelaine suggests that part of the pleasure for the original audience of *The Taming of the Shrew* lay in watching regular company members – an older apprentice actor and his master the 'company star' (whose work frequent attenders would know well) – take on the roles of Katherina and Petruccio. The older man would be teaching the younger how to be 'feminine' – but the boy would also want to impose his own ideas. Bianca, the lesser female role, would be played by a less experienced apprentice, who would understand Bianca's experience of having to wait for a chance to 'bride it' (III.2.252).

## Status

Legally, actors at the time were vagabonds, liable to the punishments Sly is threatened with – yet through their patrons they mixed with the most powerful people in the land. They were stars with a powerful fan base, yet an outbreak of plague or the censor could silence them. The edgy and exciting nature of the profession underpins the *The Taming of the Shrew*'s lively approach to pretence, change and transformation.

## Revision task 9: Playing a woman

A02

The contemporary audience would be well aware that 'Katherina' was a boy. Write about:

- How this might affect their views on the taming plot
- The expectations they might have of the player's skill

# Settings

The playhouses which first staged *The Taming of the Shrew* had no scenery. Yet this does not mean that setting was unimportant. When the playwright evoked a location in words, he gave the audience clues to the nature of the story he was unfolding: an exotic treat, set in a distant place; or a politically explosive subject, prudently set somewhere abroad; or the spectators' own England.

## Warwickshire and Padua

For the rowdier spectators, the opening of *The Taming of the Shrew* would be like looking in a mirror – a world of drunks threatened with the stocks, noisy barmaids and blood sports. However, Sly's entrance onto the balcony, surrounded with luxuries, introduces a world of fabulous wealth. The memory of 'Marian Hacket the fat ale-wife of Wincot' (Induction 2.20) begins to seem like a dream. In this play the 'real' characters (there was a real Hacket family in Wincot, close to Shakespeare's home) are replaced with professional actors evoking an exotic location.

Hence Lucentio's opening lines are an obvious theatrical device – **exposition** – to mark this shift. They underline that the play-within-a-play is not about 'real' Elizabethans but is distanced in place and perhaps time. The place names establish the glamorous setting: Lombardy, 'The pleasant garden of great Italy' (I.1.4). This was a great centre of banking: money is a theme from the outset. Padua had an ancient University, popular with English students – just the place for young men trying to better themselves, from fortune-hunting Petruccio to the clever immigrant Tranio.

## How Italian is Petruccio?

According to the text Petruccio comes from Verona. This is perhaps Shakespeare's joke, as he is indistinguishable from an Englishman. His house is at the end of a muddy road in the worst of English weather. It is a place where the servants are not called Biondello or Tranio, but 'Jacks fair within … Jills fair without' (IV.1.44) and wear the blue coats customary in England. Scenes cut entertainingly between this disorderly and chilly mansion, with rushes on the floor and meals of tripe and mutton, and Baptista's elegant Padua, where well-dressed people play musical instruments, enjoy books of Latin verse – and deceive one another.

## A free space

In Baptista's house Katherina seems stuck in her angry personality. It is not until she leaves Padua – and the scorn she encounters there – that change is possible. In Petruccio's house, however, everyone is also putting on an act. It is between these two places, in the open air, that she begins to join Petruccio's wilder fantasies. Logically this is the same road they travelled on their cold and muddy journey. But now her eyes are 'bedazzled with the sun' and everything 'seemeth green' (IV.5.47–8). In this anonymous space, Petruccio and Katherina seem at their most compatible and comfortable. Is this, perhaps, because here they are performers on an empty stage, free to improvise their relationship as they choose?

**A03** **KEY CONTEXT**

Technically Padua is not in Lombardy at all. Shakespeare is using 'Lombardy' in a rather general sense to cover a large part of northern Italy. His choice of place names is designed to evoke associations for his audience rather than to be geographically realistic.

**A05** **KEY INTERPRETATION**

In his book *The Empty Space* (1968), the director Peter Brook writes vividly about the Elizabethan stage as an instrument to explore society, what he called a 'philosopher's machine'. He locates much of its value in the basic agreement between actor and audience: 'I can take any empty space and call it a bare stage. A man walks across this empty space whilst someone else is watching him, and this is all that is needed for an act of theatre to be engaged.'

# Literary context

## The contemporary debate

Shakespeare may well have gone on rewriting *The Taming of the Shrew* for years after its first performance. Over the following four decades there were several revivals and new plays, grounded in ongoing debates about marriage and gender relationships. A sequel by Shakespeare's occasional co-writer John Fletcher, *The Woman's Prize, or The Tamer Tamed,* showed Petruccio subdued by a new bride. She induces in him the same waking dream-state experienced by Katherina in Act IV. When she finally lets him kiss her, Petruccio cries, 'Oh gentlemen, I know not where I am.'

The two plays were performed together on at least one occasion, in 1633. Other plays of the seventeenth century explored 'shrewishness' and companionate marriage. The central character of Ben Jonson's 1609 London comedy *Epicoene; Or, The Silent Woman*, the miserable Morose, seeks a quiet wife. He finds one who hardly speaks above a whisper – then turns into a screaming virago. 'She' proves to be a boy in disguise. Shakespeare's own *Much Ado About Nothing* allowed its quarrelling couple to come together in a painful situation. They then say clearly what is never quite said in *The Taming of the Shrew* – 'I do love nothing in the world so well as you. Is that not strange?'

## Modern connections

Later explorations of marriage in relation to the rights of women needed a different framework. If you compare the play to, for example, Ibsen's *A Doll's House,* you can see a shift of focus. Ibsen's concern is with the emotional and economic difficulties experienced by a woman in abandoning her dependency on a man. That possibility shocked audiences until well into the twentieth century – but it was now at least an option. Writers also continued to be interested in the dynamic between Katherina and Petruccio, which suggests quarrelling as an unconscious cover for desire. In the 1930s, for example, Hollywood produced 'screwball comedies,' where a couple fought while having adventures that left them no time to admit their love until the final moment.

Most recently, Sally Wainwright, in the BBC series *ShakespeaRe-Told*, repositioned *The Taming of the Shrew*'s characters in a modern power structure. Katherina became an abrasive MP, a potential party leader, needing a husband to improve her public image. Petruccio was a cash-strapped earl. Wainwright echoed many of the original scenes – but the new context added new meanings. Rufus Sewell's vulnerable Petruccio arrives at his wedding in a skirt – not to humiliate Katherina but to be honest about his occasional cross-dressing. At their honeymoon villa he threatens to throw her clothes into the pool unless she is 'nice'. She lets him go ahead. Then, with nothing to lose, she gives him a kiss. The play was less about 'taming' than about two eccentric people who could acknowledge their love but still had to negotiate the nature of their marriage. Hence Katherina could use the words in the original speech of submission – 'lord' and 'keeper' – but also insist on continuing her career while he looked after the children.

# CRITICAL INTERPRETATIONS

## Critical history

### Some early views

Critical comments are, of course, influenced by the theatrical performances of their time. Samuel Pepys (1633–1703) saw the play in 1667 and called it 'extremely silly' – but he was probably watching John Lacy's brutal version of the text, *Sauny the Scot*. Samuel Johnson (1709–84) enjoyed what he saw, and found 'the part between Catharine and Petruccio … eminently sprightly'. William Hazlitt (1778–1830) relished the 'bustle, animation, and rapidity of action'. For him the play 'shows admirably how self-will is only to be got the better of by stronger will, and how one degree of ridiculous perversity is only to be driven out by another still greater'. It did not occur to critics to question whether a man has a right to get the better of a woman with his 'stronger will'. George Bernard Shaw finally did so at the end of the nineteenth century, admitting to feeling 'extremely ashamed' at the prospect of listening in the company of a woman to the 'lord-of-creation moral' of Katherina's final speech.

### The twentieth century

Until the middle of the century, Shakespeare's comedies received less attention than the histories or tragedies. The focus was on his examination of government and power and on the detailed characterisation of the 'great tragic heroes'. An example is Bradley's 1904 *Shakepearean Tragedy,* which analyses the characters as if they were 'real' people.

By the 1950s, a new value was placed on the comedies. They were important because they celebrated community and the natural world. Although they might not be very individualised, the characters lived through difficulties – sometimes of their own making – for love and life to triumph. One of the famous exponents of this theory, Northrop Frye, called it 'the drama of the green world', because it moved from the bleakness of the everyday into 'the triumph of love and life over the waste land'. This reflected the rhythm of nature; it returned, of course, to winter and death, but only to blossom again.

It is clearly possible to read *The Taming of the Shrew* in this way. It ends with marriages and a feast, to which everyone is invited – even Gremio, who has no partner. Katherina undergoes a sort of death in the humiliations she endures; in the 'green world', the fresh air, where she finally submits to Petruccio, she is born again into a potentially happy relationship. Or, at least, her father refers to her as 'another daughter' (V.2.120) and gives Petruccio another twenty thousand crowns. But this, perhaps, is not quite enough to make this reading of the play convincing to us. Like most of Shakespeare's comedies, *The Taming of the Shrew* has some problems that remain unresolved. Not everyone is comfortable with a reading of Katherina which seems to put all the faults on her side. And while Christopher Sly gets a holiday in a world of pleasure and entertainment, his future looks bleak.

William Hazlitt

---

**A03**   **KEY CONNECTION**

An entertaining example of the Victorian approach to characterisation applied to *The Taming of the Shrew* can be found in Mary Cowden Clarke's 1850 volume *The Girlhood of Shakespeare's Heroines*, a collection of fifteen 'backstories' to the plays. Katherina is shown as a good-hearted girl who lacks the guidance of a mother. She and Bianca attend a convent school designed to make them into refined ladies. Katherina hates it and is constantly punished by being made to eat bread and water. Her temper almost kills a young male playmate who makes fun of her.

KEY INTERPRETATION

Early feminist critics tended to be grouped together by male reviewers who made broad generalisations about them. John Bayley, for example, said in 1982 about Marilyn French: 'Like many feminists she forces women – in her case, Shakespeare's women – to conform to her own ideas of what they should be like. Good art works differently … . Dr French may have planned a manifesto to reveal the Bard as a sex chauvinist like any other man, but what appears is just another book to show … how much the author has got out of Shakespeare.' (Review of Marilyn French's *Shakespeare's Division of Experience* in the *London Review of Books*.)

KEY INTERPRETATION

In 1986 a Turkish production of *The Taming of the Shrew* by Yurcel Enten offered a completely different approach to the comic-women-tragic-men division described here and staged the play as a tragedy. Katherina's final speech was delivered by the actress with a shawl over her arms. At the end of the speech she revealed that she had slashed her wrists, and the play closed with her death.

## Early feminist readings

Feminist critics of the late 1970s were often criticised for even attempting to relate Shakespeare to questions about women in society. Their work now looks relatively conservative. One feminist project, for example, was to rethink the study of 'character' in relation to the female roles. They explored how the women in the plays coped in a male-dominated world and they examined the relationships between female characters. This was a useful counter to the sort of criticism that perceived Katherina as a 'problem' for Petruccio to solve, rather than a woman in a society not sympathetic to her needs.

Other early feminist critics explored the plays as struggles between opposing forces. These could broadly be labelled 'male' and 'female'. Men stood for competitiveness and violence, while women represented nature and creativity. The title of one volume, Linda Bamber's 1982 *Comic Women, Tragic Men*, reflects this approach. It is an **essentialist** view, assuming that men and women have distinctly different characteristics. This view might tell us something about the expectations society places on the characters in *The Taming of the Shrew*; for instance, you could look at the roles of the older men, like Baptista, who stand in the way of Bianca and her desire to marry. However, it does not offer a helpful reading of Katherina.

A more useful critical approach was the work of Lisa Jardine. Her book *Still Harping on Daughters* explored the female roles in Shakespeare's plays, not in terms of their 'characters', but in terms of their representation on stage. She suggested that Elizabethan boy players might have held an erotic appeal for the audience. This underlines the idea that gender in the early modern period was understood rather differently, and perhaps more fluidly, than it is today.

In the light of this, it is interesting to reflect on the shifts and disguises throughout *The Taming of the Shrew*. You might turn to the Lord's instructions to Bartholomew the page about behaving like a 'gentlewoman' (Induction 1.131) with a soft voice, ready kisses and wifely tears (even if they are created by an onion). How might his performance compare to those of the boys in the troupe of strolling players who take on the roles of Katherina and Bianca? Would Katherina seem more 'masculine' than Bartholomew? How would these younger players contrast with the older man playing the Hostess?

By the mid-1980s, it was clear that there was no single 'feminist' position on the plays. It was also clear, however, that it would no longer be possible to ignore the question of gender altogether, or to take it for granted that the plays reflected 'universal truths' about human beings.

## Progress booster: The social isolation of women

Think about the roles of Katherina, Bianca, the Hostess and Sly's 'wife'. They are often socially isolated – there are no scenes of women supporting one another, while there are plenty of scenes when men do just that. Consider whether this was simply because there were fewer boy players available – or does it also tell us about women's relative isolation in their world?

# Contemporary approaches

## New historicism

This approach turns to documents of the period which have often been dismissed as ordinary or insignificant – anecdotes, sermons, letters – and uses them to illuminate better-known material. For instance, Karen Newman reads *The Taming of the Shrew* through an account of a 'skimmington' in Suffolk in 1604. This rough game was a punishment for a quarrelling couple. The wife called her husband a 'drunken dog' and beat him. The neighbours met and decided to carry him through the streets, where he was beaten again, this time by a man in woman's clothing. As Newman points out, it is worth considering this alongside the Induction. In both we see a society that believes in male dominance and punishes a 'hen-pecked' husband. But both the Induction and the skimmington contain elements of dressing-up – as if male dominance can only be maintained through pretence.

Of course, both the skimmington and *The Taming of the Shrew* ignore any injustice against the woman. The skimmington is embarrassing to the man and his wife – but nobody asks whether the wife's complaint about his drinking was justified. Likewise, Shakespeare's 'shrew' is shamed and tamed in the play acted for the drunken Sly, but nobody asks whether male-female relations could be radically different.

## Marxist criticism

The basic questions posed by Marxism are, 'Who has the power? Who makes a profit, and at whose expense do they make it?' Natasha Korda offers a way to understand the relationship between Katherina and Petruccio in terms of social class and money. Baptista is a merchant; that is, he is a member of a newly emerging class of bourgeois capitalists whose wealth is not inherited. Their wealth comes from the profits they have made in trade. Petruccio, on the other hand, is a nobleman. He has inherited his wealth from his father. As a landowner, however, he seems to live a much less affluent life.

Katherina is, as Tranio nastily points out, a 'commodity', (II.1.332), something to be disposed of for profit – the prestige of having a title in the family in exchange for hard cash. However, the emerging bourgeois class had new expectations of women. Wealthy women of an older generation would be expected to be productive, from weaving cloth to brewing beer. The new bourgeois class preferred to buy these things. A non-productive wife was a status symbol. Her chief task was to consume luxuries, like expensive clothes and rich food, in order to demonstrate how wealthy her husband was.

Petruccio, as a relatively poor aristocrat, wants a wife who does not work; but he also wants to break Katherina of the consumer values shown in her desire for the tailor's luxury goods. Her final speech, in which she speaks of the husband's 'painful labour' (V.2.155) for which the wife, safe at home, owes him the 'debt' (line 160) of obedience, suggests she has absorbed this lesson. It is, however, a lesson that renders her, and other women in her situation, less able to value herself than the 'shrews' of folk tale, who had all manner of skills if they chose to use them.

**A05**   **KEY INTERPRETATION**

Zeffirelli's 1967 production offered a reading of the play which is almost the polar opposite of a Marxist interpretation. In a long wordless sequence Elizabeth Taylor as Katherina takes charge of Petruccio's dirty and chaotic house. She rolls up her sleeves and leads the servants in a spring-cleaning operation. Clearly, this Katherina is an efficient woman with skills she is more than ready to use to create a pleasanter environment for herself.

## Revision task 10: Power and control    **A05**

Power in *The Taming of the Shrew* is in the hands of a few wealthy men. Write about:

- How the less powerful characters achieve some control over their own lives
- How they are used to the profit of those more powerful than they are

## Performance criticism

Performance study is a relatively new field, one which underlines that there is no definitive reading of a play. Not only is each production different, but the insights of the actors, the director, the designer and members of the public for a single show can offer a whole mosaic of understanding. The more productions that you can see, the more possibilities you can find in a text. If you explore past performances of *The Taming of the Shrew,* using film, reviews, photographs and comments by the director and cast, you do not only learn about the play: the production says a great deal about the period in which it was staged.

It is worth comparing, for example, Michael Benthall's 1948 Stratford production with Di Trevis's version in 1985. Benthall described his as a 'romp'; it was a practical joke on a comic drunk, who watched a show performed by a troupe of players in a rag-bag of period costumes. Katherina and Petruccio were dressed as cowgirl and cowboy and he lassoed her before carrying her off over his shoulder. Whips were cracked, custard pies were thrown and at no point did the play become serious. The production reflected the sexual conservatism of the immediate post-war years, when women were encouraged back into the home and issues like domestic violence were not publicly acknowledged.

By contrast, Trevis's version for the radical Glasgow Citizens' Theatre drew parallels between the mockery of the working-class Sly and the place of women at the bottom of the pecking order. At the end of the play, Sly came face to face with 'Katherina' the actress, a woman in rags with a baby in her arms, dragging a box of stage props behind her. Both productions emerged from the same text, but today Benthall's 'romp' seems unthinkable, and the style of Trevis's is relatively familiar to us.

## Twenty-first century interpretations

The most recent scholarship, for example the 2010 collection *Gender and Power in Shrew-Taming Narratives 1500–1700,* is well aware that *The Taming of the Shrew* continues to generate strong emotions, in a way few other plays do. It also places the play within the debates about women and 'shrewishness' running through the period. Rather than viewing the play as a piece of 'early Shakespeare', it assumes that he might have produced different versions of the text throughout his lifetime, engaging with other plays in a continuing dialogue. There are also ongoing efforts to explore the private lives of the period. While the law or the church might proclaim male power, documents suggest that women had control over medicine, food and household property. If they were often silenced, they also participated in jokes and verbal contests. It suggests that there never was, and never will be, a single *Taming of the Shrew;* it has as many different faces as its audience.

## Progress booster: Developing a personal response

This is a play which provokes strong emotions. For instance, Leah Marcus prefaces her essay *The Shrew as Editor / Editing Shrews* by describing her 'continuing rage' while reading or teaching it (see *Gender and Power in Shrew-Taming Narratives, 1500–1700*). You should find it helpful to consider your own response to the play and find critical texts which support or contradict you.

# PROGRESS CHECK

## Section One: Check your understanding

These tasks will help you to evaluate your knowledge and skills level in this particular area.

1. Consider a scene from *The Taming of the Shrew* alongside one from a play from a different period that also explores the nature of marriage.
2. What do we know about the economic status of Christopher Sly in Elizabethan society?
3. What does the play tell us about boy players?
4. Who would you describe as the most powerful person in the play, and why?
5. What setting suits Katherina best?
6. What impressions do we get of Italy?
7. How might an adaptation of the play tell you something about the period that produced it?
8. Compare two differing critical views about the scenes at Petruccio's house in Act IV and consider which better reflects your own understanding.
9. The play has been seen as reflecting the marriage debates in Elizabethan England. What questions might it have provoked among its female spectators at the time? Make a brief list.
10. What sort of effect might casting have on the way the play is understood?

## Section Two: Working towards the exam

Choose one of the following three tasks which require longer, more developed answers:

1. '*The Taming of the Shrew* is about power rather than about love.' To what extent do you agree with this statement?
2. Does *The Taming of the Shrew* offer any positive images of marriage?
3. Using examples from stage and screen performance to inform your judgement, as well as your own reading, explain how our understanding of *The Taming of the Shrew* can be influenced by the way Katherina's final speech is performed.

**A01** PROGRESS BOOSTER

For each Section Two task, read the question carefully, select the key areas you need to address, and plan an essay of six to seven points. Write a first draft, giving yourself an hour to do so. Make sure you include supporting evidence for each point, including quotations.

| Progress check (rate your understanding on a level of 1 – low, to 5 – high) | 1 | 2 | 3 | 4 | 5 |
|---|---|---|---|---|---|
| How a Marxist critic might show the rise of the new merchant class affecting gender relationships in the play | | | | | |
| How far the comedy depends upon our willingness to accept the Elizabethan view of marriage expressed in the prayer book | | | | | |
| How a feminist critic might explore the way the plot reflects a world in which women are vulnerable to the decisions of powerful men | | | | | |
| How an actor or director's decision can affect the way we view the play | | | | | |
| How different members of Shakespeare's original audience might have very different attitudes to the contemporary debates about marriage and thus to *The Taming of the Shrew* | | | | | |

## ASSESSMENT FOCUS

### How will you be assessed?

Each particular exam board and exam paper will be slightly different, so make sure you check with your teacher exactly which Assessment Objectives you need to focus on. You are likely to get more marks for Assessment Objectives 1, 2 and 3, but this does not mean you should discount 4 or 5.

If you are following an AS Level course, check the weightings carefully. Remember, there is no coursework for AS so your response to *The Taming of the Shrew* will carry even more weight in your overall result.

### What do the AOs actually mean?

| | Assessment Objective | Meaning? |
|---|---|---|
| **AO1** | Articulate informed, personal and creative responses to literary texts, using associated concepts and terminology, and coherent, accurate written expression. | You write about texts in accurate, clear and precise ways so that what you have to say is clear to the marker. You use literary terms (e.g. **protagonist**) or refer to concepts (e.g. **metatheatre**) in relevant places. You do not simply repeat what you have read or been told, but express your own ideas based on in-depth knowledge of the text and related issues. |
| **AO2** | Analyse ways in which meanings are shaped in literary texts. | You are able to explain in detail how the specific techniques and methods used by Shakespeare (e.g. recurrent symbols or motifs) influence and affect the reader's response. |
| **AO3** | Demonstrate understanding of the significance and influence of the contexts in which literary texts are written and received. | You can explain how *The Taming of the Shrew* might reflect the social, historical, political or personal backgrounds of Shakespeare or the time when it was written. You also consider how the play might have been received differently over time by audiences and readers. |
| **AO4** | Explore connections across literary texts. | You are able to explain links between *The Taming of the Shrew* and other texts, perhaps of a similar genre, or with similar concerns, or viewed from a similar perspective (e.g. feminist). |
| **AO5** | Explore literary texts informed by different interpretations. | You understand how the play can be viewed in different ways, and are able to write about these debates, forming your own opinion – for example, how a critic might view Petruccio as a swaggering bully by nature, whilst another might see him as performing the role of bully to effect a change in Katherina. |

### What does this mean for your revision?

Whether you are following an AS or A Level course, use the right-hand column above to measure how confidently you can address these objectives. Then focus your revision on those aspects you feel need most attention. Remember, throughout these Notes, the AOs are highlighted, so you can flick through and check them in that way.

Next, use the tables on page 81. These help you understand the differences between a satisfactory and an outstanding response.

Then, use the guidance from page 82 onwards to help you address the key AOs, for example how to shape and plan your writing.

Features of **mid-level** responses: the following examples relate to the relationship between marriage and money in *The Taming of the Shrew*.

| | Features | Examples |
|---|---|---|
| **A01** | You use critical vocabulary appropriately for most of the time, and your arguments are relevant to the task, ordered sensibly, with clear expression. You show detailed knowledge of the text. | *A typical lover from the **commedia dell'arte**, Lucentio seems to be uninterested in money and lets Tranio sort out the expenses. At the end of the play, however, he bets on Bianca's obedience, and **it turns out he does not really know her at all**.* |
| **A02** | You show straightforward understanding of the writer's methods, such as how form, structure and language shape meanings. | *Shakespeare uses a great deal of **imagery** about sport and games, for example hunting in the Induction. This **prepares us for the ending of the play**, when the men gamble on their wives.* |
| **A03** | You can write about a range of contextual factors and make some relevant links between these and the task or text. | ***Women in Renaissance society** were controlled by their fathers and husbands; it is not surprising that Baptista tries to arrange the marriages of both his daughters. The mercenary way he goes about this, however, would probably **alienate some of the audience** – for example, the way he keeps Gremio in reserve.* |
| **A04** | You consider straightforward connections between texts and write about them clearly and relevantly to the task. | *Shakespeare shows Katherina in a family who regard her as unmarketable, unlike her highly desirable sister who can be auctioned off to the highest bidder. In 'Much Ado About Nothing' **two women are contrasted in a different way**. The daughter of the house must marry her father's choice. Beatrice, the poor relation, can marry as she pleases. However, all the family speak highly of her wit and love her for it.* |
| **A05** | You tackle the debate in the task in a clear, logical way, showing your understanding of different interpretations. | *Some performances have **stressed the mercenary aspects** of Petruccio. In Michael Bogdanov's production he left at the end of the play with a cheque in his hand, leaving Katherina to make her own way. However, **it is also possible to see Katherina** as choosing to win the bet for her husband and becoming an asset to him.* |

Features of a **high-level** response: these examples relate to a task on conscious theatricality.

| | Features | Examples |
|---|---|---|
| **A01** | You are perceptive, and assured in your argument in relation to the task. You make fluent, confident use of literary concepts and terminology, and express yourself confidently. | *Shakespeare sets the story of 'The Taming of the Shrew' in the framework of the Induction. This means that we are always aware that we are watching what Bartholomew calls 'a kind of history'. This **metatheatrical** approach implicitly invites us to think about and judge what we are watching.* |
| **A02** | You explore and analyse key aspects of Shakespeare's use of form, structure and language and evaluate perceptively how they shape meanings. | *Shakespeare shapes this 'history' using **different comic styles** familiar to his audience. The intrigues of the **subplot** are typical of the **commedia dell'arte** and its focus on lovers' attempts to outwit the older generation. The taming plot is **linked to farce and folk-song**. However, he probes the limits of both to ask some sharp questions.* |
| **A03** | You show deep, detailed and relevant understanding of how contextual factors link to the text or task. | ***Renaissance society was patriarchal.** However, there was much debate around marriage and the theatre offered a **natural arena** in which issues could be explored. For instance, Katherina's offer to place her hand beneath Petruccio's foot would recall the **marriage service** in use previously, and might well provoke a **debate**.* |
| **A04** | You show a detailed and perceptive understanding of issues raised, through connections between texts. You have a range of excellent supportive references. | ***John Fletcher's play 'The Tamer Tamed' continues Petruccio's story.** It makes references to Shakespeare's play and gives them a **new twist**: for example, the heroine, Maria, adopts Petruccio's metaphor for the taming process, that of hawking, but declares herself a 'free haggard'. This not only indicates the popularity of the original play but suggests a desire on the part of the **audience to engage with the issues it raises**.* |
| **A05** | You are able to use your knowledge of critical debates, and the possible perspectives on an issue to write fluently and confidently about how the text might be interpreted. | ***Critics** such as Graham Holderness **suggest the play went through many revisions** in Shakespeare's lifetime and was part of an ongoing 'marriage debate'. The many shifts of identity (in Bartholomew's case, even gender) in the play make us constantly aware that labels such as 'husband', 'wife', 'wooer' and even 'shrew' and 'tamer' do not sum up a whole person, but are roles to be assumed, enjoyed, or questioned.* |

# HOW TO WRITE HIGH-QUALITY RESPONSES

The quality of your writing – how you express your ideas – is vital for getting a higher grade, and **AO1** and **AO2** are specifically about **how** you respond.

## Five key areas

<table>
<tr><td>EXAMINER'S TIP<br><br>AO1 and AO2 are equally important in AS and A Level responses.</td></tr>
</table>

The quality of your responses can be broken down into **five** key areas.

### 1. The structure of your answer/essay

- First, get **straight to the point in your opening paragraph.** Use a sharp, direct first sentence that deals with a key aspect and then follows up with evidence or detailed reference.
- **Put forward an argument or point of view** (you won't **always** be able to challenge or take issue with the essay question, but generally, where you can, you are more likely to write in an interesting way).
- **Signpost your ideas** with connectives and references which help the essay flow. Aim to present an overall argument or conceptual response to the task, not a series of unconnected points.
- **Don't repeat points already made,** not even in the conclusion, unless you have something new to add.

## Aiming high: Effective opening paragraphs

Let's imagine you have been asked the following question:

**'Comedy is about the correction of ordinary, flawed characters.' To what extent is this true of Katherina in *The Taming of the Shrew*?**

Here's an example of a successful opening paragraph:

**Gets straight to the point**

Early in the play this idea seems to be borne out by Hortensio when, hoping Petruccio will marry Katherina and free Bianca to marry him, he explains that Katherina's 'only fault' is that she is 'intolerable curst'. However, Hortensio is arguably the worst judge of character in the play, idolising Bianca, then hating her and rushing into marriage with the Widow who shows no sign of the 'kindness' he professes to value in women. While Katherina does change in the play, I would argue that to see it as the story of her comic 'correction' is to read it far too simplistically. All kinds of false ideas and false personas are demolished in 'The Taming of the Shrew' and it is important to understand how the story of her 'taming' relates to them.

**Sets up some interesting ideas that will be tackled in subsequent paragraphs**

### 2. Use of titles, names, etc.

This is a simple, but important, tip to stay on the right side of the examiners.

- Make sure that you spell correctly the titles of the texts, authors and so on. Present them correctly too, with quotation marks and capitals as appropriate. For example, *In Act II of 'The Taming of the Shrew'*....
- Use the **full title**, unless there is a good reason not to (e.g. it's very long).
- Use the term 'text' or 'play', rather than 'book' or 'story'. If you use the word 'story', the examiner may think you mean the plot/action rather than the 'text' as a whole.

## 3. Effective quotations

Do not 'bolt on' quotations to the points you make. You will get some marks for including them, but examiners will not find your writing very fluent.

The best quotations are:

● Relevant and not too long (you are going to have to memorise them, so that will help you select shorter ones!)

● Integrated into your argument/sentence

● Linked to effect and implications

## Aiming high: Effective use of quotations

Here is an example of an effective use of a quotation about Katherina's shrewishness in the play.

| short, relevant quotation, embedded in sentence | Describing Katherina to Petruccio, Hortensio says he 'would not wed her for a mine of gold'. This demonstrates the dislike for Katherina shown by all the Paduan men in the play. But it also alerts us to the way money shapes the destinies of women, and the effect of this on their behaviour. | explicit meaning / inferred meaning |

Remember – quotations can be one or two single words or phrases embedded in a sentence to build a picture or explanation, or they can be longer ones that are explored and picked apart.

## 4. Techniques and terminology

By all means mention literary terms, techniques, conventions, critical theories or people (for example, 'paradox', 'metatheatrical', 'feminism' or 'Aristotle') **but** make sure that you:

● Understand what they mean

● Are able to link them to what you're saying

● Spell them correctly

## 5. General writing skills

Try to write in a way that sounds professional and uses standard English. This does not mean that your writing will lack personality – just that it will be authoritative.

● Avoid colloquial or everyday expressions such as 'got', 'alright', 'ok' and so on.

● Use terms such as 'convey', 'suggest', 'imply', 'infer' to explain the writer's methods.

● Refer to 'we' when discussing the audience/reader.

● Avoid assertions and generalisations; don't just state a general point of view ('Katherina is an angry person'), but analyse closely with clear evidence and textual detail.

Note the professional approach here in the choice of vocabulary and awareness of the effect on the reader:

*Katherina's first appearance shows her hurling insults and making threats at those around her, but we also have some sense of her motivation: her father has made a 'stale' of her, holding her up to ridicule in front of the men who are there in order to court her sister.*

---

**EXAMINER'S TIP**

Answer the question set, not the question you'd like to have been asked. Examiners say that often students will be set a question on one character (for example, Katherina) but end up writing almost as much about another (such as Petruccio). Or they write about one aspect of the question (for example, 'correction') but ignore another (such as 'comedy'). **Stick to the question**, and answer **all parts of it**.

**EXAMINER'S TIP**

It's important to remember that *The Taming of the Shrew* is a text created by Shakespeare – thinking about the choices Shakespeare makes with language and plotting will not only alert you to his methods as a playwright but also his intentions, i.e. the effect he seeks to create.

# QUESTIONS ABOUT A SPECIFIC EXTRACT

One type of question you may come across is one that asks you to consider a particular idea or aspect in relation to an extract from the play, and then widen the discussion to the play as a whole.

For example, you might be given, Act IV, Scene 5, lines 27–58 from 'ENTER VINCENTIO' to 'A son of mine which long I have not seen'. Typical questions might relate to:

- The dramatic significance of the extract to the play as a whole, for example:

**What is the dramatic significance of this scene in terms of Shakespeare's comic design?**

- A key idea, issue or theme, for example:

**In what ways does this extract reflect Shakespeare's treatment of performance and role-play in *The Taming of the Shrew*?**

- The way a particular character or relationship is presented, for example:

**How does this scene mark a development in the relationship between Katherina and Petruccio?**

It is important from your study that you are familiar with:

- **Who** is speaking, and what you know about them **at this stage in the play**
- **Where** and **when** this passage takes place in the text (Is it the ending of a scene or act? What follows directly before and after it? Where does it take place?)
- What is **significant** about it: if you are asked about a specific issue, it is important you understand the extract's dramatic significance, even if that is not the main focus.
- How do the **specific language** and **dramatic structure** enable us to understand more about the characters/relationships, ideas/issues or dramatic significance?

So, for example, if exploring the way the passage above deals with performance and role-play you might look at:

| Key questions to focus your reading and response | Possible answers | Effect (what it tells us about the key idea/issue) |
| --- | --- | --- |
| • Who is involved/speaking? <br> • What do we know about them? | *Katherina, Petruccio, Vincentio: Petruccio has assumed a bullying persona to deal with the 'shrewishness' of Katherina. We do not know Vincentio's identity until the end of this extract.* | *Katherina addresses Vincentio with real imagination. Vincentio draws both plots together. His presence invites us to make comparisons between these performance games and the deceptions of Lucentio and Bianca.* |
| • Where and when does it take place? <br> • What has happened before this scene? | *After spending time in Petruccio's home, Katherina has yielded to him in the 'sun and moon' dispute. They are now on their way back to Padua for Bianca's wedding feast.* | *It seems fitting that she plays the game with Vincentio in a neutral space – like a stage, where roles can be assumed and discarded – not in the home where she has been stuck in the role of 'shrew' because there is little alternative.* |
| • What is significant about the scene? | *Marks a real shift in the couple's relationship. This is Petruccio's most 'unreasonable' demand, but also the one Katherina appears happiest to comply with.* | *Suggests that game-playing of the kind Petruccio does so well is different from both the suitors' disguised wooing of Bianca and the interchanges between the suitors and Katherina – maybe a sign of a healthy relationship?* |
| • What does the language and structure tell us? | *Katherina's speech is very different from her earlier angry retorts or long silences. It is the first time she uses humour which is not defensive. She outdoes Petruccio in imagery and style. Note the use of the word 'merry' to refer to Katherina – not a word previously associated with her.* | *She is co-operating with someone else for the first time, through a shared performance of an improvised scene. She picks up Petruccio's cues, but also challenges him by playing a less 'feminine' role than he expects. Her compliments are those a young man would make. Makes it clear that she is Petruccio's intellectual equal, and suggests he values this.* |

# Writing your response

There are two key things you should do when writing about an extract, once you have 'done your thinking' along the lines suggested in the table:

1. **Focus immediately** on **a specific aspect** from the scene; don't waste time with general waffle.
2. **Develop your points** succinctly and swiftly but **using inference or insight** to explore them fully.

Here is an example of an excellent first paragraph:

> *In the first words spoken by Katherina in this extract, we see how she has allowed a new side of her personality to emerge, a love of improvisation and game-playing. To show obedience to Petruccio and ensure that they continue travelling to Padua, she has only to say something like, 'Good morrow, mistress'. Instead, she launches into the sort of verse that an ardent male lover like Lucentio might use. Rather than being cowed by her husband's taming tactics, she shows she can surprise him – even, perhaps, compete in the area of language.*

In subsequent paragraphs, there are two ways to proceed:

- Work through the extract in a straightforward linear fashion.
- Take your initial point and link it to a phrase, line, etc. later in the same extract.

If you take the latter route, your response may end up moving backwards and forwards within the passage, but it will allow you to make some interesting links. For example, you might want to take one particular aspect of the idea/issue being explored and trace one character's words, then move to another character.

For example:

> *Throughout the passage Katherina and Petruccio show themselves to be accomplished performers who are also courteous. We see this in the exchange with Vincentio, when she gracefully apologises in line 46. We can infer from this that Shakespeare is contrasting them with the deceptive characters of the subplot. Vincentio will have a rough reception in Act V as a result of all the pretences in Padua.*

## Aiming high: Summarising events

Whilst it is important to understand the extract in terms of its plot significance, do not slip into simply retelling what has happened before and then telling the examiner what events are taking place now. Summarise important events swiftly and efficiently in a phrase or two, e.g. 'Once Katherina's act of obedience has allowed them to set out towards Padua ...'

> **EXAMINER'S TIP**
>
> If you have a second question to answer once you have completed your detailed response to the passage, make sure you have left yourself enough time to write fully on the remaining task.

## GENERAL QUESTIONS ABOUT THE WHOLE TEXT

Such questions might be on a key issue or idea, or on the use of language or structure, for example: '**Examine the dramatic function of hunting and sport in *The Taming of the Shrew*.**' If you are tackling this question, you need to:

● Focus on the use of hunting and sporting imagery and what it tells us about people's actions, not on their characterisation in general.
● Explain how Shakespeare **presents** or **organises** ideas about this. He frames the play in an Induction about a Lord who is a hunter; uses running metaphors of hunting, hawking and gambling; shows the taming of Katherina as if she were a hawk; presents the final outcome in terms of a wager.
● Look at the **whole text**, not just one scene or character.
● Consider **context** and **critical ideas**. For example, as this is a comedy ending in marriage, this involves looking at how the hunting and sporting imagery supports the interest in gender relationships and how this fits into the marriage debates of the day.

### Structuring your response

You need a clear, logical plan, but it will be impossible to write about every aspect or section of the play. Start by noting down five or six key ideas:

**A:** *The play uses images of hunting with hounds, of cards, archery and hawking, all competitive and male pursuits, and Petruccio uses this language too.*
**B:** *The imagery allows Shakespeare to set his play in a context where all men are hunters, pursuing rich women, but only Petruccio is honest enough to describe himself in such terms.*
**C:** *Petruccio speaks of Katherina as a 'haggard', i.e. a hawk, in a detailed way.*
**D:** *The closing scene of the play involves a bet and at least some of the audience may know enough of shrew-taming stories to expect such an ending.*
**E:** *Women and servants are both described as prey or hunter's accessories.*

Then decide the most effective order for your points (e.g. C, A, B, D, E), and draw in supporting evidence reference to context or critical ideas:

**Introduction:** *Petruccio's soliloquy in Act IV is crucial to the plot; he explains his taming strategy in terms of hawking, referring to Katherina as his 'haggard'.*
**Paragraph 1 (point C):** *This is a key speech because it makes it clear to us what is at stake. Petruccio is not just a bully, treating Katherina with random cruelty. He is applying a very specific skill. His soliloquy outlines exactly the methods of a falconer training his hawk, depriving it of food and sleep until it will obey the falconer. This method is perhaps a little risky, as we see from his appeal to the audience asking them if they know a better method.*
**Paragraph 2 (expand point C):** *This tells us something about Petruccio's character and ability to accomplish his aims: he is infinitely patient and willing to share hardship. He stays awake with Katherina and denies himself food, just as a falconer must. It also establishes Katherina as a person with valuable qualities – a falconer does not want to break the spirit of his hawk.*
**Paragraph 3 (change to Point A):** *The hawking image is just one of the sporting metaphors running throughout the play. The Lord of the Induction hunts with hounds and discusses their merits knowledgeably; in the final scene Tranio likens himself to a greyhound, let loose to hunt for his master, referring to his role in courting Bianca in disguise. He sneers 'your deer does hold you at a bay', meaning that Petruccio, unlike Lucentio, is a failed hunter. Petruccio uses an archery metaphor in pointing out to Lucentio that he has 'hit the white' (scored a bulls-eye) in marrying Bianca, whose name means 'white'. All these images suggest a society where men think of courtship itself in terms of a competitive sport.*
... and so on.

**For your conclusion:** use a compelling way to finish, perhaps repeating words from the question. For example, you might end with a final point, but add a last clause which makes it clear what you think is key to the answer:

*The sport and hunting imagery in this play includes both the complex relationship between falconer and hawk as a metaphor for Katherina's taming, and the predatory behaviour of the men, who act like hounds themselves and gamble on women as if they were animals. It offers us a multi-faceted lens through which we view relationships between men and women.*

You could also end with a quotation or aspect that is slightly different from your main point:

*John C. Bean describes Katherina in her long speech of submission as a 'trained bear'. I would suggest that she is rather a trained falcon. She retains much of her true nature, but like everyone else in the play she lives in a world shaped by predatory men.*

## Writing about context

Depending on the course you are following, you may need to focus on aspects of context that are relevant to the area you are being asked to explore. **AO3** asks you to 'demonstrate understanding of the significance and influence of the contexts in which literary texts are written and received'. This can mean either of:

● How the events, settings, politics and so on **of the time when the text was written** influenced the writer or help us to understand the play's themes or concerns.

● How events, settings, politics and so on **of the time when the text is read or seen** influence how it is understood.

The table below will help you think about how particular aspects of the time in which the play was written contribute to our understanding now of the play and its themes. For example, in relation to the question on page 86.

in relation to the question on page 86.

> **EXAMINER'S TIP**
>
> Although understanding of contexts outside the play is very important, your work should ultimately arise **from the text itself**. You need to be able to explain and explore what the text seems to be saying about a particular social or political idea in parallel with what you know of the context in which it is written or received.

| Political | Literary | Religious |
|---|---|---|
| The rise of the merchant classes (like Baptista) and corresponding shifts in attitudes to women. His exploitation of his marketable daughter, Bianca, as a trophy wife who will show off her husband's wealth rather than be a productive worker. | Use of an Italian setting and *commedia dell'arte* conventions to explore romance in a deliberately artificial way (e.g. the opening of Act I is rather stilted to show that it is a play-within-a-play). Contrast with the anti-romantic approach of Petruccio. | Protestant ideas about 'companionate marriage'. The virtue of loving fidelity makes it important that women have some say in the choice of partner. Women nevertheless expected to vow to 'obey' their husbands. Katherina's final speech sums up some of the new religious teaching of the period about marriage. |

| Scientific | Cultural | Social |
|---|---|---|
| Science of the period still shared the assumptions of classical Greek writers such as Aristotle about the biological inferiority of women. As Katherina points out in Act V, they are 'soft and weak and smooth', unlike men, who are physically and morally stronger. | Folk tales about 'shrew'-taming and their impact on the play – the audience probably expects the wager scene in Act V. The festivals that Sly alludes to in the Induction are a temporary disruption of the social order, like comedy itself. | Attitudes towards women, e.g. the Lord's instructions to Bartholomew the page, indicate some of the period's expectations that women should be quiet, nurturing and submissive. Attitudes to class, e.g. the Lord's willingness to exploit Sly for amusement, and Sly's vulnerable social status. |

## Aiming high: Making context relevant

It is very important that you do not approach context as something to be 'bolted on' to what you say. You must make fluent links between contextual knowledge and the focus of the task. For example, **don't** just write:

*Elizabethan ideas of marriage can be found in the Bible, where St Paul's Epistle to the Ephesians commands wives to submit to their husbands 'as unto the Lord'.*

**Do** write:

*Katherina's final speech, describing the duty of a wife to 'thy Lord, thy life, thy keeper' alludes to Biblical texts about marriage such as St Paul's Epistle to the Ephesians. This indicates that the sentiments would be broadly acceptable to an Elizabethan Protestant audience, although this is not to say that their response would be uncritical, any more than our own.*

# QUESTIONS WITH STATEMENTS, QUOTATIONS OR VIEWPOINTS

You may come across questions which include a statement, quotation or viewpoint that offers a particular interpretation of the text. These might be in relation to the whole text or with regard to a specific extract, and may deal with character or key ideas. For example:

> **'The tongue-lashings Katherina gives Petruccio have no other purpose than to make the audience laugh.'**
>
> **By considering Shakespeare's dramatic methods, to what extent do you agree with this view?**

The key thing to remember is that you are being asked to **respond to a particular perspective or critical view** of the text – in other words, to come up with **your own** 'take' on the idea or viewpoint in the task.

## Key skills required

The table below provides help and advice on answering the question above.

| Skill | Means? | How do I achieve this? |
|---|---|---|
| **To consider different interpretations** | There will be more than one way of looking at the given question. For example, critics might be divided as to whether the play can be seen as a farce or a complex structure which invites a more nuanced response. | Show you have considered these different interpretations in your answer through the way you juxtapose or weigh up ideas. For example: *In Shakespeare's England female silence was commended and valued, and a woman who used her tongue to scold or even question a man's will might be seen as a threat – and thus also as a caricature, a figure of fun. The slapstick episodes in Petruccio's house might suggest that Shakespeare is endorsing these sentiments in the farcical style of old entertainments about nagging wives.* |
| **To write with a clear, personal voice** | Your own 'take' on the question is made obvious to the examiner. You are not just repeating other people's ideas, but offering what you think. | Although you may mention different perspectives on the task, settle on your own view.<br>Use language that shows careful, but confident, consideration. For example: *Although Elizabethan wives were expected to promise to 'obey' their husbands, there was much debate about the nature of an ideal marriage. While this is not necessarily an ideal marriage, Katherina and Petruccio are clearly the most promising couple. I think that Shakespeare is not using either of them to evoke a single response like laughter. Rather, the speeches of Katherina, just like those of Petruccio, amuse us, shock us, and force us to think.* |
| **To construct a coherent argument** | The examiner can follow your train of thought so that your own viewpoint is clear to him or her. | Write in clear paragraphs that deal logically with different aspects of the question. Support what you say with well-selected and relevant evidence.<br>Use a range of connectives to help 'signpost' your argument. For example: *We might say that Katherina's remarks to Petruccio at their first meeting are both caustic and funny, such as her sardonic inquiry 'where did you study all this goodly speech?' However, they do more than make the audience laugh. For instance, in their opening encounter, Petruccio makes an obscene joke and Katherina strikes him. He tells her that he will strike back next time, but he makes no more jokes of that kind. Shakespeare is showing the development of a relationship, rather than simply evoking laughter. Moreover, some of Katherina's angry tirades show complex feelings ...* |

# Responding to a 'viewpoint' question

Let us look at another question:

> **'Bianca is a stereotype of female passivity in the play.'**
>
> **To what extent do you agree with this view of Shakespeare's dramatic presentation of her?**

## Stage 1: Decode the question

Underline/highlight the **key words**, and make sure you understand what the statement, quote or viewpoint is saying. In this case:

**'To what extent do you agree ...'** means: *the statement is probably valid up to a point, but there is more to be said and you need to qualify it to a greater or lesser extent according to your views*

**'stereotype of female passivity'** means: *a female character who can be seen as 'typical' of a certain kind of femininity – in this case, a woman who is an object of male desire but allows others to decide her fate*

**'dramatic presentation of her'** means: *the playwright's techniques of characterisation and Bianca's functions in the plot as a whole*

So, you are being asked whether you agree/disagree with the idea that Shakespeare is presenting us with a character we can see as a specific type of femininity, one who does not act on her own initiative.

## Stage 2: Decide what your viewpoint is

Examiners have stated that they tend to reward a strong view which is clearly put. Think about the question – can you take issue with it? Disagreeing strongly can lead to higher marks, provided you have **genuine evidence** to support your point of view. However, don't disagree just for the sake of it.

## Stage 3: Decide how to structure your answer

Pick out the key points you wish to make, and decide on the order that you will present them in. Keep this basic plan to hand while you write your response.

## Stage 4: Write your response

Begin by expanding on the aspect or topic mentioned in the task title. In this way, you can set up the key ideas you will explore. For example:

*The opening moments of Act I present us with two sisters: the noisy one and the quiet one. As Katherina the Shrew has the title role, we may assume that Bianca is presented as a clear contrast, a stereotype of the Renaissance ideal woman. However, I would argue that Shakespeare is offering us a more complex picture of her than this opening image implies.*

Then in the remaining paragraphs proceed to set out the different arguments or perspectives, including your own.

In the final paragraph, end with a clear statement of your viewpoint, but do not list or go over the points you have made. End succinctly and concisely.

---

**EXAMINER'S TIP**

You should comment concisely, professionally and thoughtfully and present a range of viewpoints. Try using modal verbs such as 'would', 'could', 'might', 'may' to clarify your own interpretation.

# USING CRITICAL INTERPRETATIONS AND PERSPECTIVES

## What is a critical interpretation?

The particular way a text is viewed or understood can be called an interpretation; it may be made by literary critics (specialists in studying literary texts), reviewers, or everyday readers and students. It is about taking a position on particular elements of the text, or on what others say about it:

### 1. Notions of 'character'

- Is the character an 'archetype' (a specific type of character with common features)? (For example, the characters in the subplot are all drawn from the **commedia dell'arte**, with stereotypical roles such as 'foolish old man' and 'clever servant'.)
- Does the character personify, **symbolise** or represent a specific idea (such as the nagging wife of folk ballads)?
- Is the character modern, universal, of his/her time, historically accurate, etc? (For example, is Baptista a typical Renaissance merchant, a modern controlling father?)

### 2. Ideas and issues

This concerns what the play tells us about **particular ideas or issues** and how we interpret them, for example:

- Themes and ideas that obsessed **Elizabethan and Jacobean** dramatists: the world as a stage; the difference between appearance and reality
- The role of men/women in early modern society and within marriage
- What **comedy** means to early modern audiences
- Moral and social attitudes towards sexuality and social class

### 3. Links and contexts

This is how the play **links with, follows** or **pre-echoes** other texts, ideas, for example:

- Its influence culturally, historically and socially: do we see echoes of the characters or genres in other texts? How similar to other clever servants is Tranio? Do we see echoes of him in the twin Dromios of Shakespeare's *The Comedy of Errors*, or a tragic version in the figure of De Flores in Middleton's *The Changeling?*
- How its language links to other texts or modes, such as religious works, myth, legend, etc.

### 4. Genre and dramatic structure

This is how the play is **constructed** and how Shakespeare **makes his narrative:**

- Does it follow a particular dramatic convention?
- What is the function of specific events, characters, theatrical devices, staging, etc. in relation to the plot?
- What are the specific moments of tension, conflict, crisis and **denouement** – and do we agree on what they are?

---

**EXAMINER'S TIP**

Critical interpretation of drama is of necessity different from critical interpretation of other modes of writing – not least because of audience response, and the specific theatrical devices in use. Key critics are theatre critics – look at what they have to say about recent productions. See the opposite margin for two examples of reviews of the 2012 Globe Theatre production of *The Taming of the Shrew*. They offer, in fact, different 'readings' of the comedy in the play and its potential to disturb or not.

## 5. Audience and critical reaction

This covers **how the play works on an audience or reader**, and whether this changes over time and in different contexts. It also includes how different types of reader have responded, from reviewers, to actors and directors, to academics and researchers. For example:

- How far do readers or audiences empathise with, feel distance from, judge and/or evaluate the events and characters?
- What ideas do they find compelling and convincing, or lacking truth and impact?
- How far do they see the play as unique and modern, part of a tradition or carrying echoes of other works and ideas?

# Writing about critical perspectives

The important thing to remember is that **you** are a critic too. Your job is to evaluate what a critic or school of criticism has said about the elements above, arrive at your own conclusions, and also express your own ideas.

In essence, you need to: **consider** the views of others, **synthesise** them, then decide on **your perspective**.

## Explain the viewpoints

**Critical view A** about Katherina's eventual obedience to Petruccio's most outrageous orders:

*Holly A. Crocker considers this an example of the way Katherina will be forced to live her life from now on, with a willingness 'to humiliate herself, even to deny her senses, in encounters similar to the scene in which she tells an old man he is a fresh maiden?'*

**Critical view B** about the same aspect:

*Jonathan Bate sees the same scene as an instance of Katherina taking control of the game. 'In a sense, she goes one up on Petruccio … a first sign that Kate can give as well as take a taming.'*

## Then synthesise and add your perspective

*While Crocker sees Katherina's obedience in greeting Vincentio as a young girl as an indication that Katherina has resigned herself to a life of petty humiliation, Bate considers it to show her dawning realisation that her ability to use language is a potential source of resistance. While I would agree with Bate that this scene does show the potential for playfulness in the marriage of Katherina and Petruccio, I think that the wager in the next scene shows the real and painful inequality between husbands and wives of the period.*

# ANNOTATED SAMPLE ANSWERS

Below are extracts from three sample answers at different levels to the same task/question. Bear in mind that these responses may not correspond exactly to the style of question you might face, but they will give a broad indication of some of the key skills required.

> Read Act III Scene 2, from Katherina: 'Nay then – / Do what thou canst,' to Baptista: 'Come gentlemen, let's go.' (end of scene)
>
> By analysing Shakespeare's dramatic methods, explore the significance of the extract to the comedy of the play as a whole.

## Candidate 1

**AO1** — Try not to repeat a word in the same paragraph

This section is important to the comedy of the play. It comes right in the middle of the play and brings the action to a climax. Then it sets up suspense about how it will all end.

**AO2** — Clear focus on question

It begins with an angry speech from Katherina. She uses proverbs in the speech which tell Petruccio to leave. Her use of clichés suggests that she is a stereotypical nagging wife of the sort the audience would find comical. Petruccio responds by pretending to be scared of her. "O Kate, content thee; prithee be not angry." This also makes the audience laugh, as he is clearly not really henpecked. Ignoring her rudeness is a part of his taming strategy. When he met her he paid her a lot of compliments about her mildness even though she was rude to him. He tells us later that he will pretend that he is keeping her without food and sleep out of love for her. He begins his taming strategy when he pretends to defend Katherina against everyone else on stage. I think he is doing it for another reason as well – to make her think what a loving person would be like.

**AO2** — Give examples to make the point more clearly. It could be shaped into a good argument about how Shakespeare uses language

**AO1** — Rather chatty style here

**AO5** — A sound point and a good understanding of the play, but needs to be related to the question. Could discuss this as an aspect of Petruccio's characterisation (AO2), or in relation to some ideas of comedy

Petruccio does a lot of comic things in this extract. He takes centre stage and is rude to everyone in an over-exaggerated way. He tells them they are 'thieves' and accuses them of going to the feast to get drunk and behave madly. He was late turning up, he behaved badly in the church and now he refuses to go to his own wedding feast and drags Katherina away. This gives a lot of scope for slapstick comedy, especially at the end where Petruccio and Grumio pretend to fight. Everyone on stage will be involved, either watching or maybe even fighting if Petruccio or Grumio actually attack them. It is important to note that they have not seen this side of Petruccio before and their surprise will be comic for the audience. Katherina does know that he can act in ways that seem weird. She even told her father he was marrying her to a lunatic, but he ignored her. Now Katherina says, 'Father, be quiet', which suggests that Baptista is trying to speak but is having trouble finding something to say because he is so flustered. This is amusing, as Baptista is usually very controlling, telling his daughters what to do and making a profit out of the suitors by letting them organise tutors for Bianca. Everyone ends up laughing at Katherina as she is carried off, including Bianca, who says she is 'mad herself, she's madly mated'. This is typical of

**AO1** — A good point but a little vague. Cite some text, and discuss possibilities in performance style

**AO2** — Helpful point with good focus on Shakespeare's method

**AO2** — Good point, but needs to be made more relevant to the question – could discuss the use of non-verbal comedy and how the playwright gives the actors opportunities for comic reactions

**AO2** Not really relevant to the question – but could be made so by discussing the ending and relating the point more clearly to the structure of the play as a whole

Bianca, but Lucentio does not know that yet. She gets Katherina's place at the feast, just like she always gets the best of everything.

Petruccio's bad behaviour has another reason, it shows Katherina what she is like when she is shrewish. For instance, she dragged Bianca about with her hands tied, just like he is dragging her off to his house. He goes on behaving like this at his house, he shouts at the servants and the tailor and even hits people, as Katherina has done. Shakespeare is creating the sort of comedy described by Aristotle, which is about ordinary people with ordinary flaws in their characters – nothing evil or wicked, but foolish and not knowing themselves very well. When people laugh at them they are taught to do better. I think this is happening here for Katherina, it is very painful for her to be 'made a fool', especially in front of people like Gremio who have been unkind to her. They all assume that she will go on being a shrew for ever, as when Gremio says 'marry, sir, now it begins to work.' She stamps and frets, but Petruccio tells her, 'I will be master of what is mine own.' He goes on to quote from the Bible, showing her what a wife's place is. Katherina will learn to change. She does not say very much after Petruccio has made this speech about her being his 'chattels' and she will go on being silent in the next Act. Shakespeare is preparing a surprise for the end, when she makes a very long speech that also contains material from the Bible, showing she has learned from Petruccio.

**AO5** Some grasp of comic theory which has been usefully applied – needs some development

**AO2** Other readings of this are possible – show awareness

**AO2** Good knowledge of play, but relate this point more to dramatic method

**AO3** Some sense of context, but it needs to be developed here

**AO3** Generalised reference to historical context – needs to be developed

**AO2** These are valid points, but they need to be more carefully focused towards the question. There is an attempt to bring the answer to a conclusion, but it leaves several loose ends

I think Shakespeare meant us to think that this is a happy ending and that Petruccio is doing all this to help Katherina. Women in the period had a very hard time and were expected to obey their husbands even if they were violent. Petruccio is not really violent. He is only pretending here, but I find it uncomfortable to watch as Katherina does not get to choose her husband. In this part she does not want him at all, although earlier in the scene she was upset he had not come to marry her, so she did want to marry someone. Later she calls him 'love', so we are meant to think she is happy.

**AO5** Asserts a personal view – worth developing this argument, which arrives rather late in the answer

### MID LEVEL

**Comment**

- AO1 The material covered is broadly relevant but sometimes it is left to the reader to work out why. A tendency to narrate the story rather than relate it to the question.
- AO2 Has a grasp of some comic theory and applies it, e.g. the discussion of the correction of Katherina. Some well chosen quotations. Some grasp of the visual comic potential and an evident engagement with the play. Slightly clumsy discussion of the ending to conclude the answer, which needs to be made more directly relevant to this extract.
- AO3 Attempts to put the play in its historical context. Identifies Biblical source for a speech and talks in broad terms about marriage in the period.
- AO4 Does not really mention other comic texts for comparison.
- AO5 Does not cite critical perspectives on the text, but does show awareness that different interpretations are possible.

**To improve the answer:**

- Focus on commentary rather than narration. Explain the relevance of some of the points, e.g. the discussion of Bianca, which could be made into a discussion of contrasts rather than a point about her character. (AO1)
- Make more use of the text to offer specific examples, including closer analysis of the extract, e.g. develop the comment on Katherina's use of proverbs. (AO2)
- Develop more complex sense of context – it would help to see the play as part of a debate in its era rather than expressing a single point of view. (AO3)
- Examine another comic text for useful comparison, for example *Much Ado About Nothing*. (AO4)
- Include some critical perspectives and consider different points of view. (AO5)

## Candidate 2

**A01** Clear start

This extract comes at the end of the third Act, often a crucial turning point in Shakespearean comedy. It marks the end of the first part of the action – the intrigues that allow Bianca and Lucentio to fall in love and want to marry, and Petruccio's negotiations to marry Katherina for twenty thousand crowns. It also starts off a new phase, in which we will see the taming strategy followed up and the marriage of the other couples.

Because it is an important section Shakespeare brings together most of the characters for a scene of memorable comedy. Petruccio's ridiculous clothes and the mock fight will evoke laughter and provide an exciting exit, which will also create suspense about what happens next.

**A01** Starts to focus on question more tightly

**A01** Introduces the main point of the argument

However I think Shakespeare is also using this episode to show us something new about the characters of Katherina and Petruccio, which ties in with his theme of real and false love in the play. At the beginning of the scene Katherina was angry and disappointed when Petruccio failed to arrive; that was the first suggestion that she would perhaps like to be married to him. Now they are married Katherina wants the dignity of a bride at the head of the table – the way she addresses the guests as 'gentlemen' when telling them to go to the feast shows this. When Petruccio refuses to go she shows the same anger she showed to Hortensio and Gremio at the start of the play. Petruccio is not ruffled by this. He agrees that she can order the guests to the dinner but that she must go with him. She is silent for the rest of the scene. This is an important change for Katherina. She has always stood up for herself, but everybody ignored her. Now Petruccio takes notice of her, but is also setting boundaries. The silence suggests that she is shocked. She will not be confidently talkative again until the end of Act IV, after the argument about the sun and the moon – in other words, she will only talk when she has learned to cooperate with Petruccio, however ridiculous his orders.

**A02** Could relate more closely to the question with more detail about Katherina's development as comic heroine

**A02** Good obervation

**A02** Promising line of argument, but it would help to give more precise analysis of how this is shown in the extract

**A02** Broad statement – more support with quotation would help

**A05** Introduces critical opinion effectively

However, I agree with the critic Alexander Leggatt that Petruccio is not being cruel but paradoxical – his behaviour is teaching her that social conventions like this feast matter to her more than she thinks. Shakespeare balances this section to make Petruccio's actions show this. On the one hand is he polite to Katherina, asking her not to be angry and telling everyone to 'obey the bride' as if he recognises she has rights. On the other hand he is rude to everyone else. He shouts at them as if they did not know how to behave at a feast and accuses them of wanting to kidnap his 'bonny Kate'. He is doing this to make his quarrelsome bride long for a more orderly life. But it may also reflect his opinion of the other characters' hypocrisy. They are not happy for Katherina. Gremio sneers as if he thinks the marriage is a joke,

**A02** Good points, but they need to be more carefully laid out rather than run together – the argument is slightly blurred here

**A02** Add quotation to support this

**A03** Indicates knowledge of religious context but is a little undeveloped

Bianca and Lucentio play at tutor and pupil, and Baptista seems glad to be rid of her. When Petruccio invokes the Bible by calling Katherina 'my goods, my chattels' he is doing two things. He is letting her know that she is a wife now. At weddings in Shakespeare's time a wife promised to 'obey'. But he is also saying to the others that he is serious about this marriage, and implying that they are not.

**A02** Could relate this to your overall point about the ending

**A02** Develop the point a little – this seems to be about a bond between them, but it isn't quite clear

The way he behaves is comic, ranting and waving a sword in his absurd clothes, but it also makes us think. We know that he likes to perform and show off – his pompous speech in the first act about hearing 'lions roar' makes this clear, just as Katherina's rude rhymes about Hortensio at her first entrance in the play show that she is using her shrewish persona to deal with the cruel jokes that come her way. Petruccio's play-acting dramatises to Katherina how unpleasant her shrewish ways can be, but when he shouts at the wedding guests as he carries her off it also shows her that performing can be fun. Performing her speech at the end of Act V allows Katherina the freedom to puncture the self-satisfaction of her sister, and make Hortensio, who has always been rude to her, lose his money. I think that throughout this episode Shakespeare is dropping hints about the nature of relationship he will explore later. At the end of the play Katherina and Petruccio have something real between them. The others do not. Although they may make romantic speeches, Bianca and Lucentio are an image of false love and it is significant that in this scene Lucentio is dressed as someone else and Bianca grabs a chance to 'bride it' at Katherina's expense. At the end I think that we see Katherina and Petruccio in harmony, an image of a real if unromantic love that makes the play a true comedy.

**A01** Need to have a paragraph break – this is a new point

**A03** Good visual point – could pay more attention to what we see as well as hear

**A01** Returns to the question to finish the answer – a neat conclusion

GOOD LEVEL

**Comment**

- AO1 A well-structured answer with good knowledge of the text
- AO2 Awareness of comic structure and good location of this scene within it. Does not always explain the relevance of its discussion of other scenes.
- AO3 Some attempt to place this in historical context, correctly identifying Biblical quotation and discussing its significance in this section.
- AO4 Does not discuss other texts.
- AO5 Introduces critical perspective deftly.

**To improve the answer:**

- Make each point clearly rather than running some different observations together because they are about the same topic. (AO1)
- Relate points about the play as a whole more directly to the extract to sharpen the presentation of the arguments. Consider the visual aspect of the text more closely – what characters do is often as important as what they say. Explain the relevance of some points more clearly. (AO2)
- Develop the discussion of context, e.g. to consider Elizabethan attitudes to women in general as well as wives. (AO3)
- Explore some other texts, for example about quarrelling couples who fall in love. (AO4)
- Introduce some critical perspectives you can argue against, rather than using them only to support your own viewpoint. (AO5)

## Candidate 3

**AO1**
Begins at once with a broad statement that sets up its main line of argument

This sequence marks a key point in Shakespeare's comic structure. It unites the characters from both plots for an energetic climax to the action so far. It then raises questions to keep us in suspense about how a resolution will be achieved.

**AO2**
Quotations well chosen from other parts of the text to support the argument

**AO3**
Insight into how the marriage plot links with historical conventions

Fittingly for a major sequence, Shakespeare weaves together the different comic methods he employs throughout the play. The most obvious of these is farce, as Petruccio and Grumio 'defend' Katherina against the Paduans. The spectacle they present in their ridiculous clothes is fully exploited; Petruccio's 'old rusty sword' and the puny stature of the 'little pot' Grumio suggest their fighting techniques will evoke laughter. However, although this scene has been played as broad slapstick (Edith Evans was carried off on a pantomime horse) Shakespeare gives it a satirical edge. Petruccio radically disrupts this wealthy and rather smug society. Earlier – in the church for example – his antics humiliated Katherina. In this sequence, however, he seems more interested in ridiculing the Paduans. In the first scene they made a 'stale' of Katherina, deriding her failure to marry; here they perhaps anticipate the bridal dinner as an opportunity for bawdy jokes at her expense – Elizabethan wedding celebrations were notoriously ribald. Instead they receive a Puritanical diatribe from Petruccio – 'be mad and merry or go hang yourselves' – as if they, not Katherina, were the unmannerly ones. Their dismayed reactions offer the actors comic opportunities – especially for Baptista, who must be wondering what sort of son-in-law he has paid for. Although once the stage is safely clear of the anarchic couple, the wedding guests claim they were ready to 'die with laughing', the audience has observed and enjoyed their discomfiture. Petruccio's words and actions here divide the community into opposing sides – Petruccio and his 'bonny Kate' against these hypocrites who may talk about love, but treat women (to use Tranio's term) as a 'commodity'. He may be a fortune hunter, but this refusal to conform to Paduan values is refreshing. If we recall Katherina's anger and isolation in Scene 1, we may begin to envisage a bond between this unlikely couple. Shakespeare is preparing us for the final scene, which sharply contrasts the unity of 'outsiders' Petruccio and Katherina to the 'loving' couples bickering at their own feast.

**AO2**
Good focus on variety inherent in a particular comic method

**AO2**
Clear focus on the question – ensures whole paragraph is seen to be relevant

**AO1**
Leads well into a new line of argument

In contrast to this bustle, Shakespeare employs the commedia dell'arte conventions of the subplot for quieter, more sophisticated laughter. Here the success of Tranio's early intrigues reach a logical conclusion, one that may comically disconcert Lucentio. In his disguise as a lowly tutor he has to address his beloved respectfully as 'mistress', while watching his own servant – wearing his own fancy clothes – treated deferentially as Bianca's wealthy fiancé. As Baptista invites the disguised Tranio to 'supply the bridegroom's place', Lucentio may react involuntarily and have to stifle a reply; worse, he hears Tranio flirtatiously referring to 'sweet Bianca' as he goes to his place at the feast beside her, the seat that should be Lucentio's. Lucentio's attempts to repress his jealousy and remember his schoolmaster role will provide much silent comedy, and anticipate his subsequent disillusionment

**AO2**
Good awareness of the playwright's craft – looks at the text as a blueprint for performance

with Bianca. Katherina's wedding also removes any reason to delay Bianca's. The audience will now be in suspense to see whether the clever servant can find a 'father' for his master up his sleeve.

**AO5** Good use of a critical viewpoint which it goes on to challenge with its own nuanced reading

For Katherina this is a painful episode, as her tirade against Petruccio suggests. I agree with Susan Bassnett that 'The Taming of the Shrew' is a 'problem play'. However, I believe that if 'comedy' means 'a story with a happy ending' Katherina is better off at the end of the play. This sequence is an important turning point for her character. It marks the beginning of a shift from her entrenched position as angry, unwanted outsider into a partnership. As her final speech in the play indicates, this is an Elizabethan marriage where the wife 'obeys' the husband, but it does contain the possibility of love. Petruccio's insistence that she can 'command' others to the feast but not go herself, and his Biblically-based description of her role as 'my household stuff ... my anything' assert his marital authority, and this is painful for her. Alongside this, however, comes an unspoken invitation to join a game: a parody of romantic chivalry as he cries 'touch her whoever dare'. Petruccio's enjoyment of paradox and play-acting, so evident here, is something Katherina finally chooses to share by teasing Vincentio in Act IV – and the wit she shows in praising the 'young budding virgin' suggests she enjoys herself. In this extract she is – unsurprisingly – too shocked and bewildered to participate. But the rescue game is, literally, her way out of Padua and its mean-minded values. It completely negates Baptista's treatment of her as a waste product to be disposed of before he can market Bianca. Here, as throughout, Petruccio describes Katherina as an object of desire, one Gremio and co. might want to steal. Shakespeare makes him use such language throughout the taming process, thus modifying its darker aspects. Petruccio never disparages Katherina. This lets us see his 'sweet wench' as the heroine of a comedy of love rather than a misogynist stereotype.

**AO3** Puts extract in context of the play and the play in its historical context. Could develop this argument

**AO5** Open-minded approach which acknowledges that a text may embody more than one viewpoint

**AO2** Discusses the comic design of the whole, rather than sticking to the viewpoint of a single character

**AO2** Relates the extract to the whole play and identifies specific dramatic method

**AO1** This follows logically from the overall analysis, but could have been introduced earlier

Simplistic comedy confirms stereotypes. Complex comedy makes you see the world differently. I believe with Graham Holderness that in this play Shakespeare is joining the marriage debates of his era. By using so many comic styles – farce, commedia, anarchic games – and calling attention to them by framing the whole story with the Induction to make a comedy-within-a-comedy, he makes us laugh, but also ensures we think about what we are laughing at.

**AO1** This follows logically from the overall analysis, but could have been introduced earlier

**AO1** Brings us back to the question and offers a fresh concluding point

**VERY HIGH LEVEL**

### Comment

- AO1 Fluently written and clearly structured
- AO2 Good knowledge of the text – chooses quotations from the extract well and quotes relevantly from the rest of the play. Interprets the visual aspects of the scene in some detail and pays useful attention to all the characters, not just those taking centre stage.
- AO3 Shows awareness of a wider context, notably the marriage debates of the time.
- AO5 Useful references to critics and not afraid to take issue with them at times. Good use of comic terminology which is closely related throughout to dramatic method.

# PRACTICE TASK

Now it's your turn to work through an exam-style task on *The Taming of the Shrew*. The key is to:

- Quickly read and decode the task/question
- Briefly plan your points – then add a few more details, such as evidence, or make links between them
- Write your answer

## Decode the question

> 'Although the play is a comedy, Shakespeare's presentation of gender relations undermines the laughter.' By considering Shakespeare's dramatic methods, to what extent do you agree with this view?

| | |
|---|---|
| **'comedy'** | suggests that you need to discuss comic form and the expectations it creates |
| **'gender relations'** | suggests that it is important to look at all aspects of male-female relations in the play, not just those between Petruccio and Katherina |
| **'undermines the laughter'** | suggests that you need to discuss the darker aspects of the play and relate them to comedy. Do we sometimes laugh but feel uncomfortable doing so? |
| **'dramatic methods'** | suggests you must focus on what Shakespeare *does* – not just language, but also structuring of events, for example |
| **'to what extent do you agree?'** | What is my view? Do I agree with the statement completely, partially or not at all? |

## Plan and write

- Decide your viewpoint
- Plan your points
- Think of key evidence and quotations
- Write your answer

### Success criteria

- Show your understanding of the two key ideas as aspects of audience response
- Draw on a range of critical views or different interpretation as appropriate
- Sustain your focus on the idea of 'gender relations' and 'undermining laughter'
- Argue your point of view clearly and logically
- Make perceptive points and express your ideas confidently
- Support your points with relevant, well-chosen evidence, including quotations
- Use literary terminology accurately and appropriately with reference to the effect on the reader
- Write in fluent, controlled and accurate English

Once you have finished, use the **Mark scheme** on page 112 to evaluate your response.

## FURTHER READING

### The text and its sources

Barbara Hodgdon, ed., *The Taming of the Shrew* (The Arden Shakespeare), Methuen 2010
    The edition of the text used in the preparation of these Notes

Linzy Brady, Rex Gibson, Vicki Wienand, Richard Andrews, Diane Clamp, Michael Fynes-Clinton and Perry Mills, eds., *The Taming of the Shrew* (The Cambridge School Shakespeare), Cambridge University Press, 2014

Jonathan Bate and Eric Rasmussen, eds.,*The RSC Shakespeare: The Complete Works*, Palgrave Macmillan 2008

### Criticism

Susan Bassnett, *Shakespeare: The Elizabethan Plays,* Macmillan 1993
    Usefully explores how the play tests the limits of comedy and relates it to Shakespeare's other early work.

John C. Bean, 'Comic Structure and the Humanising of Kate in *The Taming of the Shrew*', in *The Woman's Part: Feminist Criticism of Shakespeare*, eds. Carolyn Ruth Swift Lenz, Gayle Greene, Carol Thomas Neely, University of Illinois Press, 1980 (1985)
    One of the early volumes of feminist criticism

Stevie Davies, *The Taming of the Shrew* (Penguin Critical Studies), Penguin, 1995
    A feminist examination of all aspects of the text

Frances E. Dolan, ed., *The Taming of the Shrew: Texts and Contexts*, Bedford Books of St. Martin's Press, 1996
    Includes the text of the play and extracts from Renaissance texts on marriage, the household, shrew-taming.

Juliet Dusinberre, *Shakespeare and the Nature of Women*, Palgrave Macmillan, 1975
    Discusses the plays in relation to changing attitudes to religion and the family.

Penny Gay, *As She Likes It: Shakespeare's Unruly Women*, Routledge, 1994
    Helpfully explores the play in performance.

Penny Gay, *The Cambridge Introduction to Shakespeare's Comedies,* Cambridge University Press 2008
    Different theories of comedy and the comic genres in *The Taming of the Shrew*

Graham Holderness, 'Text and Performance: *The Taming of the Shrew*', *Shakespeare in Performance* Palgrave Macmillan, 2000
    A history of the play in production, with interesting comments on *The Taming of the Shrew* in comparison with *The Taming of A Shrew*

Lisa Hopkins, *Beginning Shakespeare,* Manchester University Press, 2005.
    Very clear introduction to varieties of literary theory and how they can be applied to Shakespeare

Lisa Jardine, *Still Harping on Daughters: Women and Drama in the Age of Shakespeare*, Harvester Press, 1983
    Looks at the historical context and explores the effect of boy players.

Alexander Leggatt, *Shakespeare's Comedy of Love*, Methuen, 1974
    Looks at the contrasts of style in the play and at the use of dreams.

Laurie Maguire, *Studying Shakespeare: A Guide to the Plays,* Blackwell 2004
    An illuminating approach to the analysis of Shakespeare's characters in their political and social context

Michael Mangan, *A Preface to Shakespeare's Comedies 1594–1603*, Longman, 1996
    A helpful introduction to how Shakespeare's audience understood jokes and laughter

Carol Rutter, *Clamorous Voices: Shakespeare's Women Today*, Routledge, 1989
    Valuable interviews with some noted actresses who have played Katherina

David Wootton and Graham Holderness, eds., *Gender and Power in Shrew-Taming Narratives,* Palgrave Macmillan 2010
    Includes essays by Leah Marcus and Holly Crocker, and explores the marriage debates in the sixteenth and seventeenth centuries.

Marion Wynne-Davies, ed., *Much Ado About Nothing and The Taming of the Shrew* (New Casebooks Series), Palgrave Macmillan, 2001
    Includes essays by Karen Newman, Lynda E. Boose and Natasha Korda

### General reading

Douglas Brode, *Shakespeare in the Movies,* Oxford University Press 2000

John Fletcher, *The Tamer Tamed,* Nick Hern Books for the Royal Shakespeare Company, 2003

Andrew Gurr, *The Shakespearean Stage*, Cambridge University Press, 1992

Michael Hattaway, *Elizabethan Popular Theatre,* Routledge 1982

Samuel Schoenbaum, *Shakespeare: A Documentary Life*, Oxford University Press, 1975

Lawrence Stone, *The Family, Sex and Marriage in England 1500–1800*, Weidenfeld & Nicholson, 1977

Peter Thomson, *Shakespeare's Professional Career,* Cambridge University Press 1992

Stanley Wells, ed., *Shakespeare in the Theatre: An Anthology of Criticism*, Clarendon Press, 1997

# LITERARY TERMS

**aside** common dramatic convention, in which a character speaks in such a way that some of the characters on stage do not hear what is said, while others do.

**ballad** (French 'dancing song') poem or song which tells a story in simple, colloquial language. The subject matter of ballads is often violent. During the Elizabethan period ballads were accessible to most people; they were sung in the streets by their sellers, and mass produced. There were a number of comic ballads about shrewish wives.

**blank verse** unrhymed verse often (though not always) in iambic pentameter (see below).

**comedy** a broad genre which encompasses a large variety of different kinds of literature; however, 'comedy' is used most often with reference to a kind of drama which is intended to entertain the audience, and which ends happily for the characters.

**commedia dell'arte** (Italian 'comedy of the professional actors') a form of drama that evolved in sixteenth-century Italy in which travelling companies of actors improvised comic plays around standard plots, using stock characters. A typical play might involve a young lover, the 'Inamorato', tricking Pantaleone ('Pantaloon'), a rich old father, into giving up his daughter. Arlecchino ('Harlequin'), the cunning servant, and Pulcinella ('Punch'), the hunchback clown, were other stock types.

**climax** the high point of the action.

**dramatic irony** a feature of many plays: it occurs when the development of the plot allows the audience to possess more information about what is happening than some of the characters on stage. Characters may also speak or act in an ironic way, saying something that points to events to come without understanding the significance of what they say.

**epilogue** concluding speech or passage in a work of literature, often summing up and commenting on what has gone before.

**essentialism** the view that people and objects have certain characteristics that are essential to them and are not accidental.

**exposition** the opening sections of a play in which information vital to the understanding of the plot is conveyed to the audience.

**farce** (Latin 'to stuff') drama intended primarily to provoke laughter, using exaggerated characters and complicated plots, full of absurd episodes, ludicrous situations and knockabout action. Farcical episodes date back to Aristophanes and occur alongside serious drama in all ages.

**feminist, feminism** broadly speaking, a political movement claiming political and economic equality of women with men. Feminist criticism and scholarship seek to explore the masculine 'bias' in texts and challenge traditional ideas about them, constructing and then offering a feminine perspective on works of art. Since the late 1960s feminist theories about literature and language, and feminist interpretations of texts have multiplied enormously.

**figurative language** any form of expression or grammar which deviates from the plainest expression of meaning is designated 'figurative language'. Departures into more decorative language are further defined by a large number of terms. **Metaphor** is probably the figure of speech which most clearly characterises literary language: hence 'figurative language' can specifically refer to metaphorical language as well as to language abounding in other figures of speech.

**foreshadowing** a device used to suggest what events are to come.

**humanist** in the Renaissance, a scholar of the humanities, especially classical literature. The humanists' attitude to the world contrasts with the religious view in centring upon humanity for its own sake rather than treating humankind as a fallen creature who must look to God for goodness; their idea of truth and excellence is based on human values and human experience.

**iambic pentameter** a line of five iambs (a light stress followed by a heavy one). One of the commonest English metres, it was introduced into England by Henry Howard, Earl of Surrey, and became the normal medium for verse plays because it fitted the rhythms of spoken English.

**imagery** the **figurative language** in a piece of literature (**metaphors** and similes); or all the words which refer to objects and qualities that appeal to the senses and feelings. Thematic imagery is imagery (in the general sense) which recurs through a work of art: for example, images of card-playing, hunting and hawking are all invoked in *The Taming of the Shrew* to suggest the way in which the male characters relate to women.

**induction** the prologue introducing a work.

**irony** saying one thing while you mean another. However, not all ironical statements in literature are that simple; the overall patterns– of situation, character, structure and vocabulary – need to be carefully looked at and the writer is probably assuming that the audience share certain values and attitudes.

**metaphor** (Greek 'a carrying over') goes further than a comparison between two different things or ideas by fusing them together: one thing is described as being another thing, thus 'carrying over' all its associations.

**metatheatre** theatrical style which calls attention to itself and reminds us we are seeing a play.

**motivation** the underlying reason for an action. A term much used by actors to explain their character's decisions.

**new historicist, historicism** the work of critics who discuss literary works in terms of their historical contexts. In particular, they study literature in relation to other kinds of documents from the period.

**protagonist** the central character in a play.

**pun** a 'play on words': two widely different meanings are drawn out of a single word, usually for comic, witty or playful purposes.

**resolution** the tying-up of all the threads of the plot to reach a satisfactory conclusion.

**rhetoric** the art of making speeches, an art studied at Renaissance universities.

**slapstick** broad comedy with knockabout action, fighting, clowning, people falling over each other.

**soliloquy** convention which allows a character in a play to speak directly to the audience, as if thinking aloud about motives, feelings and decisions.

**stereotype** clichéd image of a common type of person.

**stichomythia** a dialogue carried out in single alternating lines.

**symbol** something that represents something else (often an idea or quality) by analogy or association.

# REVISION TASK ANSWERS

## Revision task 1: How important is the Induction?

- Retain – the Induction frames the two plots. It reminds us that they are both fictions – 'a pleasant comedy' (Induction 2.126) – and invites us to read them critically.
- Retain – the Induction alerts us to themes developed in the main plot – transformation, class difference.
- Expand – the audience will want to know what happens to the likeable character of Sly.
- Expand – the play was presumably designed to conclude with a scene about Sly and it is worth adding material to fit this.
- Cut – modern audiences will already consider the 'happy ending' of the play to have come from another era and read it critically.

## Revision task 2: Family ties

- BAPTISTA: 'Was ever gentleman thus grieved as I?' (II.1.37) – has one daughter he thinks he will never marry off. His house is disturbed by Katherina's anger and by the quarrelling of his daughters.
- BIANCA: 'Sister, content you in my discontent.' (I.1.80) – cannot marry until her sister does. Despite her popularity with men, she is kept at home and sees few people. Katherina ties her up and bullies her. Her father sees her as a marketable asset, and is not interested in her feelings.
- KATHERINA: 'is it your will / To make a stale of me among these mates?' (I.1.57–8) – is paraded as a potential wife in front of men who want her sister. The men hope that for a price someone can 'rid the house of her' (I,1,144). Bianca exploits her status as angelic favourite with remarks like, 'So well I know my duty to my elders' (II.1.7). Her reputation as 'Katherine the Curst' (I.2.127) precedes her: she is never seen by anyone without the label already attached.

## Revision task 3: Romantic speeches

- Petruccio confides his strategy of relentless compliments to us, so we expect his praise of her sweet nature; he may be providing a running commentary on what the Katherina actor is actually doing, so that 'Thou canst not frown' (II.1.249) responds to an actual scowl.
- The extended comparison with hazel twigs and hazelnuts is rather different. If he is continuing to be ironic, one might expect praise of her fair hair or white skin.
- Katherina's speech is an act of obedience. But the language is more suited to a dashing young man than a meek wife.
- Both are more extravagant with language than the occasion warrants – but in both cases the 'extra' they bring to the task is harmless, not hurtful. Vincentio is puzzled. Petruccio expresses unconventional liking for Katherina's style of beauty.
- In both their speeches, they are not so much mocking as pleasing each other – perhaps unconsciously.

## Revision task 4: Silences

- When she enters Petruccio's house in Act IV Scene 1, Katherina is cold, tired, and has no idea what to expect from the man she has married on his home ground. There is much to look at, with a crowd of unfamiliar servants and a chaotic meal.
- After she expresses approval of the gown (IV.3.103–5) Katherina is silent while Petruccio shouts at the Tailor and Grumio.
- This is difficult for an actress: first, a comic row she cannot join, then a sermon about clothes. She cannot seem too crushed, as the scene ends with a new argument. Shakespeare offers her no help here – perhaps she should be unobtrusive.
- Her final exit. She has no lines, but her body language will dictate our response to the ending. Is she embracing Petruccio? Trailing behind as he leaves?

## Revision task 5: Unreality

- Lucentio opens Act I with a speech that suggests a player in the 'comedy' arranged by the Lord. It outlines not just the information we need, but the fact that it is a piece of exposition.
- It tells us that Lucentio is a conventional *commedia dell'arte* lover. We expect him to fall in love, and to depend on his servant – he does.
- Katherina is described by one of Petruccio's servants as 'one new risen from a dream' (IV.1.175). This suggests how to play her in the scenes at Petruccio's house: confused and disconcerted.
- It implies her situation is temporary – Petruccio will not subject her to this treatment for ever.
- Vincentio assumes that Katherina and Petruccio 'break a jest' (IV.5.73) in treating him like a young woman and perhaps in their news of Lucentio. This suggests that their manner is playful – that they bond over their enjoyment of fantasy.

## Revision task 6: Madness

- 'Stark mad' (I.1.69): Tranio's diagnosis on seeing Katherina's rudeness to the suitors – but the way she is paraded in front of them deserves her scorn.
- 'half lunatic' (II.1.290): Katherina's assessment of Petruccio after his wooing. He is parodying conventional romantic tactics – although she will not appreciate this at the time.
- Petruccio's arrival in disorderly clothes for his wedding: this disconcerts Katherina, but his insistence (here and in Act IV) that clothes do not make the man contrasts with and critiques the materialism associated with Bianca's wooing.
- Petruccio's antics in the church (III.2.156–81): like those of a 'madman', but also a criticism of the rowdy enjoyment of the wedding guests, who may well want to see Katherina humiliated.

- His pretence of carrying her off after the wedding: part of his taming strategy, but it is also an implied critique of Bianca and Lucentio, who will also run away – and whose marriage will prove that they do not really know each other.

## Revision task 7: Two weddings

- KATHERINA'S: creates suspense as to how the marriage itself will play out; launches the taming process with Petruccio's insistence on leaving before the feast.
- Delayed start makes Katherina acknowledge desire to be married – and commitment to social order in that she wants an orthodox wedding.
- It reveals the malicious side of the Paduans, who treat it as a joke.
- BIANCA'S: the wager at the feast is expected by an audience familiar with the folk tales about taming. Provides a spectacular setting for Petruccio's triumph.
- Katherina shows loyalty to her husband, even reciting a kind of marriage service. Bianca reveals the reverse, letting Lucentio down.

## Revision task 8: Playing yourself

- In the first encounter between Katherina and Petruccio, they communicate through puns and wordplay. Each is determined to have the punch-line of the joke, and will start up a new train of thought to keep control of the language.
- The snappy rhythms – they often share a pentameter – suggest that they enjoy the competition, like tennis players enjoying a rally.
- It is usually Katherina who initiates an insult which Petruccio then deflects. Not with a view to silencing her – pauses only occur when one of them breaks the unspoken rules of the game (his obscene remark, her blow to his face).
- When Katherina first appears, she is paraded by her father like an unsaleable horse. Taunted by Hortensio, she makes the most of the attention. She pretends he might conceivably want her and rejects him in stinging rhyme. Carefully chosen words like 'noddle' (I.1.64) diminish his attempt to look like a polished wooer of Bianca.

- Petruccio's boast to his friends in Act I: imitating the heroic figures in plays like Marlowe's *Doctor Faustus,* he shows his own skill and brings that convention down to earth, typical of his anti-romantic performance style. He's competing with the classical scholar Lucentio on his own ground with all those allusions – arguably winning here as he wins his bet at the end.

## Revision task 9: Playing a woman

- They will be slightly at a distance from the action and may respond critically rather than getting involved in their feelings towards Katherina.
- They will be aware that the plot is old-fashioned and perhaps hope for a new twist, such as Petruccio's relative humaneness.
- The play foregrounds the question of playing and it may prompt the reflection that gender is a construct or disguise, rather than an immutable aspect of personality.
- The boy player will be expected to offer an image of female attractiveness through movement and voice – to be a worthy reward for the hero.
- He will project a generalised image of women.

## Revision task 10: Power and control

- BIANCA uses passive aggression – 'content you in my discontent' (I.1.80) – and duplicity to get her own way.
- SLY makes some attempt to play along with the Lord's trick, shifting into verse and adapting his manners – there are some material rewards in this.
- TRANIO gets the fun of wearing rich clothes and courting a wealthy woman.
- BIANCA is auctioned off to the highest bidder.
- THE LORD derives entertainment from his trick.
- PETRUCCIO gains a dowry for taking Katherina, another for taming Katherina, and a hundred crowns for betting on Katherina.
- In none of these cases does anyone question the ethical position of the powerful.

# PROGRESS CHECK ANSWERS

## Part Two: Studying *The Taming of the Shrew*

### Section One: Check your understanding

**1.** What tricks are played on Christopher Sly in the Induction, and why? Write a list of the tricks and suggest the Lord's possible motives.

- Sly is dressed in fine clothes, given rich food, led to think he is a nobleman who has been deluded for fifteen years, and that he has a wife.
- The Lord's chief motive seems to be to play a practical joke.
- However, there may be a punitive element – he sneers at him as 'like a swine' (Induction 1.33).
- He also seems to relish the idea of playing with Sly's idea of reality, anticipating that he will see his experience as a dream.

**2.** What differences, if any, do you note in the behaviour of the Minola family when no outsiders are present?

- Baptista treats his daughters in much the same way, disparaging Katherina and indulging Bianca, whether in private or in company. However, he never speaks to either of them about marriage plans privately – he lets others do it
- Bianca always shows an obedient face to her father, whether others are present or not. Although her behaviour is arguably the most devious in the play, she never actually speaks of it. The only time she is alone with Katherina, she does appear to speak her mind about her suitors.
- Katherina speaks freely at all times, but only when alone with Bianca does she address her at all.

**3.** Why do Lucentio and Tranio exchange clothes, and how do you think this affects their behaviour? Write notes outlining your viewpoint.

- They change clothes so that Lucentio can woo Bianca disguised as a tutor and Tranio can negotiate a marriage settlement.
- Tranio becomes even more confident in his expensive clothes. He irresponsibly bids outrageous sums of money for Bianca. He also flirts with Bianca at Katherina's wedding feast.
- Tranio demands the arrest of Vincentio – a risky strategy. Has power gone to his head?
- Lucentio successfully courts Bianca by revealing his identity. However, the disguised suitors are remarkably rude to each other; are they taking a break from the need to act like gentlemen?

**4.** How would you describe the relationship between Petruccio and Grumio? Write notes explaining your viewpoint.

- Their relationship is longstanding – Grumio is an 'ancient, trusty, pleasant servant' (I.2.46).
- Petruccio beats him – does this suggest oppression?
  YES: Grumio cannot risk striking back.

NO: it may be mainly play-acting – the 'knock me' jokes of Act I are shared humour.

- Grumio is trusted to co-operate in the taming strategy – against his will?
  YES: he says he 'dare not' offer Katherina food.
  NO: he engages in so much word-play when she is asking him for food that he is clearly in sympathy with Petruccio's aims and enjoys helping him.

**5.** How would you describe the first encounter between Katherina and Petruccio? List some words that would fit a comic view, and some that would fit the reverse.

- COMIC: banter, word-play, speed, mutuality, rhythm
- NOT COMIC: inequality, authority, enforcement

**6.** The last Act of a comedy often involves weddings, but here all the marriages have already taken place. Make notes on the effects this has on our view of the relationships between the couples.

- Overall focus is anti-romantic; whether marriage is a 'happy ending' depends on the couple.
- The behaviour of Bianca and Lucentio is not endorsed – rather, their courtship is shown to be a poor basis for marriage.
- Is it a problem that Katherina does not consent?
  YES: in the end it remains a forced marriage – we would prefer to see her as free to choose. The traditional story precludes this and is no longer acceptable to us.
  NO: focus is on negotiation of a relationship within the confines of marriage, something many women in Shakespeare's audience would understand.

**7.** What does Petruccio have to say to the audience on the subject of taming Katherina, and why does he think he can do it? Make brief notes on his techniques.

- At the close of Act IV Scene 1 he explains that he will treat her as a falconer does his hawk – keeping her hungry and sleepless.
- He is speaking here as an expert falconer – and treats the audience as if they are too – 'as we watch these kites' (IV.1.184).
- He will also persistently assert that his angry rejection of his servants' housekeeping shows his care for her.
- This particular pretence means her anger will have to be deflected away from him – he will 'kill her with kindness' until it is curbed (see line 197).
- This is risky – his appeal to the audience at the end of his speech suggests confidence, but not total certainty.

**8.** How do the other men in the play describe Katherina? List four or five examples.

- Tranio: 'stark mad' (I.1.69) – also a term he uses of Petruccio
- Gremio: 'fiend of hell' (I.1.88) – a reaction to Baptista's keeping him from Bianca?

- Hortensio: 'Katherine the Curst' (I.2.126), a catchy phrase taken up by Grumio and Petruccio, but also 'young and beauteous' (I.2.85) – bear in mind when forming any mental picture of Katherina.
- Baptista (to Petruccio): 'she is not for your turn' (II.1.63) – the least kind of all his strictures, implying he would only marry Katherina to someone he did not like.

**9.** Name some strategies the suitors use to pursue Bianca. Which do you think she finds most gratifying?

- Gremio and the disguised Tranio offer enormous wealth – she does not express much interest in money when discussing suitors with Katherina.
- Hortensio in disguise as a tutor attempts to play the lute and to declare his desire in a musical exercise. She does not like this at all. Could she have seen through the disguise and be tormenting him?
- Lucentio presents himself as a Latin master and declares his feelings under the guise of translation. Bianca uses this as a good opportunity to flirt and try out her power over Lucentio. This works very well for her and she gets the man she wants.

**10.** What financial arrangements are made around the marriages of the sisters? Make brief notes to show how these indicate each sister's relationship with her father.

- The disguised Tranio offers: three or four houses; land worth two thousand ducats a year; three argosies; two galliasses; twelve galleys.
- Baptista's concerns are: Vincentio to ratify this; Bianca's dowry must not revert to Vincentio if his son dies before him.
- Baptista keeps Gremio in reserve as a second choice – he does not seem to care who Bianca marries.
- He agrees that Petruccio shall have twenty thousand crowns and half of his lands when he dies.
- It is left to Petruccio to discuss what happens if Katherina is left a widow and to ensure it is all legally arranged.
- Baptista also mentions 'the special thing' (II.1.127), Katherina's love. This sits oddly with his other remarks – but perhaps it is important for the audience to be alert to the possibility of love.

**11.** Find three statements to show Petruccio's financial interest in Katherina. Do you think these interests are compatible with a happy marriage?

- 'I come to wive it wealthily in Padua' (I.2.74). Thanks to *Kiss Me, Kate*, this is seen as a sort of theme song for Petruccio.
- 'if I get your daughter's love / What dowry shall I have with her to wife?' (II.1.118–9) This is brisk and to the point, but at least seems to open up the possibility of consent.
- 'your father hath consented / That you shall be my wife, your dowry 'greed on' (II.1.271–2). Whatever we think of Petruccio, he is the only person to talk directly to a woman about the financial side of marriage.
- NO: this is not compatible with happy marriage – he equates money with his own happiness.
- YES: it is compatible – he has taken trouble to make provision for Katherina and is always honest with her, never pretending to feel more than he does.

**12.** What are the chief differences between Katherina's journey to Petruccio's house and her return to Baptista's? Write your ideas in a two-column table.
*Could include:*

- Journey to Petruccio's: cold, wet, muddy roads; Katherina's horse falls on her – Petruccio ignores her; Petruccio shows ill-temper; Petruccio beats Grumio
- Return to Baptista's: sunny day; party on foot and all together; Petruccio insists on conformity, but expresses approval when he gets it; Petruccio and Katherina tease Vincentio.

**13.** Describe the experiences of Vincentio and the Merchant in the play. Who do you think has the more difficult time? Make brief notes.

- The Merchant: is told that as a Mantuan he is in danger of execution; once disguised he seems to take command of the house; when Vincentio is identified, he beats a very hasty retreat – is he afraid?
- Vincentio: is addressed as a girl by Katherina and Petruccio; hears the news of his son's marriage from strangers; is treated as a 'madman' by Baptista and the Merchant; is nearly arrested at the behest of Tranio; when he sees Tranio in his son's clothes, he suspects he has been murdered.
- Arguably Vincentio's experience is the more uncomfortable, but the conventions of farce mean that he – like the others – does not try to sort things out rationally.

**14.** Petruccio and Katherina both have detailed descriptions of off-stage incidents involving horses. What effect does this have on their next appearance on stage? Write brief notes on each incident and its effect.

- Petruccio: he arrives for his wedding on a spectacularly broken-down horse. A build-up to his own entry in ridiculous clothes.
- The opposite of a status symbol, the horse underlines his sermon about the unimportance of appearance.
- Katherina: Petruccio lets her flounder in the mud when she falls off – to teach her about travelling side by side?
- Her experience will probably show in her clothes for the next Act.
- This reinforces her desire for the new ones Petruccio does not allow her.

**15.** What tasks does Tranio have to do in order to make Bianca's marriage with Lucentio possible? Make a short list.

- Explain the condition Baptista has made about Katherina marrying first.
- Present himself as Lucentio to Baptista and bid for Bianca.
- Act as her fiancé in public at Katherina's wedding.
- Arrange for Hortensio to eavesdrop on Bianca and her 'tutor' and encourage Hortensio to renounce her.
- Find a 'father' to agree the dowry.
- Play host at his lodgings to Baptista and the Merchant as they make the arrangements.
- Keep the deception going until the secret marriage is accomplished.

**16.** What does Hortensio learn, or not learn, from Petruccio? Write brief notes exploring the progress of their relationship.

- The two are old friends – this is perhaps why Hortensio sees him as a possible suitor for Katherina.
- Petruccio instructs him on the importance of 'gold'. Is this why Hortensio eventually settles for a rich widow?
- At the 'taming school' Hortensio is quiet – impressed by Petruccio? Helpfully advises Katherina that if she doesn't agree about the time of day, they will never leave for the feast.
- Over-confident at the feast about the Widow's obedience and rude to both Katherina and Petruccio – Hortensio seems to have missed Petruccio's point somehow.
- Petruccio is cutting about Hortensio's marriage – it looks as if the friendship has eroded.

**17.** List three ways Petruccio tests Katherina's obedience in the course of the play. How do their outcomes differ? Write your ideas in a two-column table.

*Could include:*

- The 'sun and moon' argument: Katherina agrees to whatever he says.
- Greeting Vincentio as a girl: she does this better than Petruccio.
- Kissing in the street: shy – but then calls him 'love'.

**18.** What impression does Act IV give us of Petruccio's home? Write brief notes.

- It is very English – cold, wet surroundings.
- There's a pet dog.
- It is quite simple – rushes on the floor, servants in plain clothes rather than fancy livery – although Petruccio is a gentleman.
- The servants are quite simple people. Petruccio knows them all by name.
- They seem accustomed to serving well – Grumio is clear about his tasks – and the disorder is temporary.

**19.** How are material objects used to create comedy? Choose six and write a sentence about each one.

- Bartholomew's dress: he has to be instructed how to behave in lady-like fashion, so may wear it with comic awkwardness.
- Hortensio's lute: he may well appear as described, with his head framed by the broken lute (although lutes were expensive, and the company would not have wasted the real thing).
- Lucentio's Latin text: there is much illicit flirting around this – perhaps the book itself is large and makes a handy screen.
- Hortensio's 'gamut': music masters often guided the hands of their students when teaching gamut. Perhaps he hopes to touch Bianca's – and perhaps she finds ways to stop him.
- Mutton: Petruccio criticises it and may throw a joint of meat when they arrive at his house. Later he offers meat to Katherina, but gets Hortensio to eat most of it.
- Katherina's gown: Petruccio abuses it at length verbally and perhaps rips it up – it was probably made to get some laughs about current fashion.

**20.** What are the main points Katherina makes about how women should behave, in her final speech?

- Women should not show resentment towards their husbands.
- They should respect a man's role as breadwinner – obedience is his reward.
- Women are weaker physically – this suggests that they should be submissive.

## Section Two: Working towards the exam

**1.** Explore the different functions of clothing in the play.

- Clothing is linked to truth and falsehood.
- Disguise: Hortensio and Lucentio dress as tutors to court Bianca. It allows them the freedom to approach her – but they are so busy using their persona to flirt they learn nothing about her.
- Tranio disguises himself as Lucentio and becomes increasingly cocky. He overreaches himself with the attempt to arrest Vincentio.
- Do clothes make the woman? Katherina's relationship with clothes is complex. The cap and gown are withheld until she is 'gentle' – as if she's being constructed as 'feminine', like Bartholomew the fake wife – but Petruccio also tells her clothes are unimportant.
- Do clothes make the man? Petruccio announces 'To me she's married, not unto my clothes' (III.2.116) – but he puts on special clothing to make the point.
- Tranio says that Petruccio often goes 'mean-apparelled' (III.2.70) – Petruccio may be in revolt against the flashy falsehood of the Paduans. He may make Katherina 'gentle' but also wants to stress that they are both different from the Paduans.

**2.** 'The sexual politics of *The Taming of the Shrew* make it impossible to enjoy as a comedy.' Do you agree?

- YES: women are commodities. Bianca is sold – her deceit to get her way may amuse us, but the social structure is unchanged.
- YES: Katherina has no choice in marriage beyond 'like it or lump it' and the text makes no arguments against this.
- YES: although Petruccio is not actually violent, his behaviour often edges close to it, especially in Act IV.
- YES: Katherina's 'place your hands below your husband's foot' (V.2.183) indicates a marriage of extreme inequality.
- NO: the Induction gives a distance and the plots are familiar enough to be seen as 'old-fashioned' – they are not meant to reflect contemporary Elizabethan attitudes.
- NO: the wordplay and games between Katherina and Petruccio at their first meeting and on the way back to Padua suggest growing attraction.
- NO: Katherina moves from unwanted daughter to a wife whose husband values her. Her final speech contains elements of the marriage service, suggesting she consents freely.

3. What is the value of the subplot?

- Contrasting worlds: artificial, *commedia* plot evoking a place of glittering deceit, versus a rough English country integrity – we are invited to decide what we value.
- Contrasting sisters: prompt the audience to think about what a woman/wife should be.
- Constant suspense: as we shift from one setting to another. There is usually a 'cliffhanger', for example Katherina's wedding night and Petruccio's soliloquy are followed by a new twist in Bianca's machinations.
- Skill: at first the two strands of the plot seem quite separate; the way they are drawn together is satisfying to watch.
- 'our jarring notes agree' (V.2.1): Lucentio's comment invites us to consider two marriages side by side; without the insight provided by the wager scene, we cannot judge the changed Katherina in a social setting.

4. *The Taming of the Shrew* is a play within a play. How might that affect the way the audience responds to it?

- Sly's expectations of 'a Christmas gambol or a tumbling trick' (Induction 2.134) may give them a sense of their own sophistication – they may be in a more reflective frame of mind.
- If the Lord, Sly and Bartholomew are present as 'audience', the spectators will be watching their responses.
- This in turn will affect theirs, e.g. if Sly shows approval of the rougher elements, they may withdraw their own.
- They may focus on the physical comic skills of the performers, e.g. Petruccio's servants, rather than being perturbed by the potential for violence.
- Heightened awareness of the boy players – may lead them to consider 'femininity' and what is expected of women.
- Awareness that the Shrew plot is an old one – they may think their own attitudes to marriage are more 'modern' – Katherina's final speech would be an insight into the bad old days, not 'realistic'.

5. 'The play is essentially anti-romantic.' Do you think the way it depicts the relationships between the three couples bears out this statement?

- YES: even the runaway couple, Bianca and Lucentio, are a good match from their fathers' viewpoint. There's no real sense that love can cross social boundaries.
- YES: Hortensio slanders Bianca's virtue when it's clear she loves another and marries the Widow out of pique.
- YES: Petruccio never declares love for Katherina – he 'comes to wive it wealthily' (I.2.74) and that is what he does.
- YES: at least two husbands seem to regret their choice.
- NO: the play is suggesting that love can grow within marriage. This is not unromantic.
- NO: there is a focus on female choice. Petruccio's behaviour on the wedding night means that he does not consummate the marriage – he waits for Katherina to show her willingness. She does so through her kiss to him in the street.
- NO: Petruccio and Katherina are typical of the witty couples in Shakespeare's comedies of love – this time, the man is the wittier of the pair.
- NO: although it does not end with her wedding like a conventional romantic comedy, in her long speech Katherina is effectively performing her true wedding vows.

## Part Three: Characters and Themes

### Section One: Check your understanding

1. Who in the main plot do you think shares character traits with Christopher Sly?

- Petruccio: similar convictions about a man's right to dominate (but has more success); shares some of Sly's countrified style – his house could be part of Sly's own world.
- Katherina: resists being dominated; shares the dream-like puzzlement of Sly when he enters his new environment, and his underdog status.

2. What does Petruccio say about himself? Should we take it seriously?

- He says he is 'a gentleman of Verona' (II.1.47) and his status is confirmed by everyone.
- He claims a heroic past, involving lions and battles – a parody of popular tragedies like *Tamburlaine*. We may assume he is showing off for fun.
- He says 'I come to wive it wealthily in Padua' (I.2.74) and does consistently show an interest in money (although this does not mean it is the only reason he chooses Katherina).

3. What do the other characters think of his methods of taming Katherina?

- The Servant Peter: 'He kills her in her own humour' (IV.1.169) – the servants understand he is mirroring her behaviour, and co-operate.
- Tranio: sees him as a 'master' (IV.2. 57) of a successful 'taming school' (55) and evidently admires his technique.
- Hortensio: on the road to Padua says, 'the field is won' (IV.5.24) – but is sceptical at the wedding feast. Perhaps he never quite gets the point.
- Baptista: never asks questions about how the transformation has been achieved – perhaps he does not care.

4. 'Madness' is a recurring theme in the play. Find three instances of the word and make notes exploring the different senses in which it is used.

- Tranio: 'That wench is stark mad' (I.1.69) suggests he might think a woman must be unstable to defy her father and suitors.
- Katherina: labels Petruccio as 'a mad-brain rudesby' (3.2.10) when he does not arrive on time for the wedding. Here, the word implies a capricious taste for practical jokes. Reflects her lack of trust – and suggests she values courtesy more than she thought.
- Petruccio: 'how now, Kate, I hope thou art not mad' (IV.5.43) – he knows she isn't, and is following his own orders to greet Vincentio as a girl. Is this a joking reference to the way others have disparaged her? She picks up the word herself a few lines later.

5. Money and material goods are indicators of how Katherina and Bianca are valued in their society. Make a table for each of

them showing what they are considered to be worth – and what they cost the men in their lives.

*Should include:*

Bianca:
- Hypothetical valuation: 3 or 4 houses; land worth 2000 ducats a year; 17 assorted ships. (We do not know how much of this is delivered.)
- Actual costs to others: cost of tutor (borne by Gremio); 1000 crowns bet by Lucentio.

Katherina:
- Original valuation: negative; 2000 crowns removal fee
- Cost to Baptista: dowry; replacement lute?; second dowry
- Profit to Petruccio: dowry; second dowry; 1000 crowns x 2

**6.** Education is a theme in both the plot and the subplot. What are the differences in the 'lessons' taught?

Subplot:
- Music lesson 'teaches' Hortensio's desire – also his inadequacy as romantic lover, as he can neither attract the girl nor play a tune.
- Latin lesson 'teaches' Lucentio's intentions – also, teaches Bianca a useful formula for keeping him in suspense through mischievous translation.
- Nobody actually learns much about themselves or one another.

Main plot:
- Value of order through presentation of disorder.
- Justice – Katherina intercedes when Petruccio berates servants for innocent mistakes.
- 'The poorest service is repaid with thanks' (IV.3.47).
- Difference between appearance and reality – Petruccio is constantly concerned with clothing and what it fails to show about the person.

**7.** Money shows how a man fits in his society – usually through the way he spends it. Choose five items mentioned in the text which indicate a man's social position, and arrange them in order of prestige.

1. Art: The Lord's pictures create a magical world – in it Sly loses all sense of self.
2. Hawk: Petruccio sees himself as creating his wife in this image – it's the most valuable living creature.
3. Clothes: Tranio's outfit as Lucentio endows him with enormous confidence and Vincentio sees it as a possible motive for murder.
4. Hounds: the Lord values these hugely – as Petruccio also does – but leaves their management to others.
5. Horse: can be a major status symbol. Petruccio is aware of this, and subverts the idea – anything gets him from A to B.

**8.** Find three instances of deception and explain how it is achieved.

- Sly is convinced he is a lord by surrounding him with luxury and treating him with deference. The Lord perhaps plays on his secret longing for a better life.
- Biondello is convinced that the Tranio/Lucentio swap is necessary by telling him that Lucentio has killed a man. (It is not clear why – this is a measure of his credulity.)

- Hortensio is convinced that Tranio is actually Lucentio and shares his pain at Bianca's 'unfaithfulness' with her 'tutor'. This is an easy task – he only has to watch a brief staged scene – perhaps because he is not really in love.

**9.** What are the characteristics of a good servant? Do any of the servants in the play fit the bill?

- Domestic servants keep a house clean and welcoming. Petruccio's seem to understand this well, and their chaotic behaviour is not normal. Perhaps they are happy to indulge him – Peter grasps his motivation.
- Personal servants help with advice, care of clothes, organising their master's time and keeping them out of trouble. Tranio is very efficient at this, although he may go too far in gratifying his own desires.
- Grumio is equally efficient at both personal and household service, but takes far more liberties by commenting on Petruccio's sanity and answering back.

**10.** The subplot is full of romantic lovers: what are the rules that shape their courtship?

The man should:
- offer extravagant compliments
- play music (or order it to be played)
- find ways to be with his lady, even if it is forbidden
- accept any changes in his lady's mood or desire

The woman should:
- keep her lover in suspense
- change her mood to keep him on his toes
- be chaste
- be beautiful in a conventional way
- embody ideals of femininity, not be original

## Section Two: Working towards the exam

**1.** Suggest the reasons why Hortensio and Gremio fail to get the women they want.

Gremio:
- never actually speaks to Bianca– he finds it only logical to go through Baptista: 'I am your neighbour, and was suitor first' (II.1.338).
- pays 'Cambio' to do the work of wooing for him – it doesn't occur to him that a handsome young man might be a threat.
- is convinced that money is the way to get a bride.

Hortensio:
- doesn't attend Bianca's 'auction' at all – has he not thought about this?
- is not a very accomplished courtly lover – he is no good at music and spends most of his time with Bianca sniping at 'Cambio'.
- does not understand Bianca, drawn only by her 'beauteous looks' (IV.2.41).
- abandons Bianca as soon as he has a clear rival – perhaps he only likes the idea of love.

**2.** *The Taming of the Shrew* hints at the future lives of three married couples. Based on your understanding of the characters, say what you think these marriages will be like.

Bianca and Lucentio, the pair who chose freely:

- He sees a wife as something to 'achieve' (I.1.155).
- She is fond of attention.
- Lucentio does not give her much attention at the wedding feast. He may not be very attentive now she is 'achieved'.
- She resents being ordered about and being the subject of a bet – a lot of resentment is being stored up between them.

Hortensio and The Widow, settling for second best:

- He sees the marriage as a reward for her love – does not love her?
- They can both be spiteful (notably to Katherina at the feast), which is a bond, but it may turn sour.

Petruccio and Katherina, an unromantic match:

- Based on money, but no lies – Petruccio never pretends otherwise.
- Both natural performers – they may be able to entertain each other (as they do in the Vincentio episode).
- Inequality – Katherina has had no choice and her final speech suggests acceptance of this. He is not violent to her, keeps his promises.
- In an Elizabethan Protestant context, a workable marriage.

**3.** 'Being mad herself, she's madly mated' (III.2.245). Explore the theme of 'madness' in the play in relation to men and women.

- We should not assume any speaker uses the term accurately – right at the start, Sly is told that his real life has been a madman's delusion.
- Katherina is labelled 'stark mad' (I.1.69) when all she has done is show justified resentment of the way the men treat her – do the men equate 'madness' with 'not being like Bianca'?
- Petruccio is called 'mad', but only by his social inferiors: a woman – Katherina calls him 'half lunatic' (II.1.290) – and a servant, Grumio.
- They are, in a sense, right – his wild behaviour is an act (rather as Hamlet's is); do the wellborn men refrain from agreeing out of gentlemanly solidarity? They would not want to suggest that a gentleman can't do anything he likes.
- For Petruccio the label will not have the painful consequences it would have for Katherina or Sly. His 'mad' persona is like the licensed folly of a jester – in the teasing of Vincentio he encourages Katherina to share this 'madness'.
- When the marriage is labelled 'mad' – by Gremio, Bianca, and Tranio – it is seen as a joke. For Petruccio, however, it is a way of liberating Katherina from Padua and conformism, even while he insists on curbing the 'mad' humour that makes her violent.

# Part Four: Genre, Structure and Language

## Section One: Check your understanding

**1.** What features mark the play as a comedy? What sort of comedy?

- Stock *commedia* characters – the Pantaloon, the Lovers, the Servant

- Slapstick episodes
- Characters with slight flaws, who learn from experience
- An emphasis on festivity, and a love story that ends in marriage

**2.** From what the characters say, what are the characteristics of a 'devil'? Make a brief list.

- Female: Katherina is so described by Gremio and Hortensio in I.1.
- Angry: she is called so for expressing her rage at being paraded by her father to be rejected by them.
- Violent: Baptista uses the label for Katherina after she ties up Bianca.
- Frightening: Hortensio prays to be delivered 'From all such devils' (I.1.66).
- Talkative: a woman's tongue is the devil's instrument, so they repeatedly silence Katherina.

**3.** How does Christopher Sly respond to the food given him by the Lord's servants? What does his response tell us about him?

- When offered 'sack' (sherry), he demands 'small ale' – the weakest and cheapest from a tavern. He rejects 'conserves' (salted beef – very expensive).
- Suggests that his tastes have been shaped by his social class – he is not used to luxuries.
- This may just be reluctance to try something new – but as the servants are all trying to convince him he is somebody else, it is also a way of hanging on to his identity.

**4.** What sports feature in the play and what do they tell us about the people who play them? Write your ideas in a two-column table.

*Should include:*

Hunting with hounds (and betting on them):

- the Lord – though his men do much of the work
- Petruccio – we know that he gambles, but is not especially interested – perhaps it is not subtle enough

Coursing with greyhounds:

- the Lord
- Tranio, though only metaphorically – sees himself as Lucentio's 'hound' to hunt women for him

Hawking:

- the Lord – offers Sly the chance
- Petruccio – his real sport, needing skill

Betting on wives:

- Petruccio, Hortensio, Lucentio

**5.** Which characters are the targets of slapstick comedy, and what kind of impact does their physical experience have on them? Write your ideas in a two-column table.

*Should include:*

- Grumio: beaten by Petruccio and Katherina but does not take it seriously.
- Katherina: servants upset food or keep it out of her way – this disorientates her.
- Hortensio: hit off-stage with the lute and may come on wearing it – confirms his feelings about Katherina.

**6.** The lovers in the play use poetic language – does this reflect their true feelings?

- Lucentio speaks about Bianca's beauty – which is fair – but also calls her 'Minerva' (I.1.84) and 'sacred and sweet' (I.1.175). He has no idea what she is like yet, so he has to rely on conventional language.
- Hortensio's 'gamut' in III.1 states that he will die for love but he instantly rejects Bianca when he sees her evident desire for 'Cambio' – not how a courtly lover should behave.

**7.** The play alternates between plot and subplot to increase suspense. List some moments you might describe as 'cliffhangers' and note the questions the audience might be asking themselves.

- Petruccio's exit after his first meeting with Katherina – will she go through with the wedding?
- At the end of III.1, Hortensio announces he will investigate 'Cambio' – Bianca's relationship with Lucentio may be thwarted.
- The end of Katherina's wedding focuses on Bianca – we are waiting to see how Katherina will find married life.
- The time-of-day dispute in IV.3 – will they ever get on the road to Padua?
- Biondello arranges Bianca's wedding in V.1, followed by the dispute between the Merchant and Vincentio – if this is resolved too soon, Gremio may work out what is happening and the wedding may not take place.

**8.** Which characters use language associated with work, and why? Write your ideas in a two-column table.

*Should include:*

- The Lord: shows off his knowledge of hounds.
- Huntsman: it is his job – perhaps he knows more than the Lord, but can't say this.
- Biondello: knows horses, so he comes to life here; a comic set piece.
- Grumio: lists tasks for the servants in Act IV – clear understanding shows the disorder is temporary; offers an image of the harmony Petruccio is aiming for.
- Tailor: pride in his craft – the destruction of the gown hurts him; satirises fashion, but also teaches Katherina that abusive language can do harm.

**9.** The text suggests that Katherina and Bianca differ greatly in looks and dress, as well as in manner. Write notes on each character with this in mind.

Bianca:
- Name means 'white' which suggests a blonde.
- Coral lips, according to Lucentio (I.1.173) – a conventional beauty.
- In II.1 Katherina is pulling at Bianca's 'goods', suggesting her clothes are covered in ornaments and jewels.

Katherina:
- Even Hortensio says she is 'beauteous' (I.2.85).
- Petruccio compares her to a hazel twig and a hazel nut (II.1.255) – a slim, dark woman who stands up straight – not fashionable, but not unattractive.
- Goes through a great deal on her wedding journey – suggests that she is muddy and that her clothes may be torn, especially as she's keen for a new gown.

**10.** The physical appearance of *commedia dell'arte* characters is often based on animals. Which characters are compared to animals, and what does it suggest about them? Write your ideas in a two-column table.

*Should include:*

- Katherina: shrew (throughout) – linked to the devil, small and fierce; hawk – Petruccio treats her as one – his inferior but highly valued; fierce and wild, and must not be otherwise.
- Petruccio: 'more shrew than she' (IV.1.76), a tribute to his originality in choosing to behave in a way more associated with the female.
- Gremio: 'An old Italian fox' (II.1.406), he has too much sense to trust young men with money, though he does not really have foxy cunning.
- Bianca: bird (V.2) – flighty, and also vulnerable
- Tranio: greyhound (V.2) – hunts for his master. Perhaps a rather bitter summary of all he has been through to help Lucentio.

## Section Two: Working towards the exam

**1.** Comedy is often concerned with characters who learn social lessons – or who fail to do so. Which characters in *The Taming of the Shrew* do you consider to have learned nothing at the end of the play, and why?

- Aristotle suggests that comedy shows ordinary people with ordinary flaws. We laugh at them, and sometimes they learn to do better.
- Some characters here remain stuck in their ways – notably the ones who make Katherina's life a misery.
- Hortensio sees Petruccio as a role model, but in Act V is rude to Katherina, despises Bianca, and is married to a woman who lets him down. A simple misogynist?
- Baptista is happy to pay Petruccio a bonus, but has nothing to say to Katherina, assuming he has nothing to feel guilty about.
- Lucentio – knows little about Bianca, and is beginning in Act V to regret his marriage. Failed to take his opportunity to learn about the beloved.
- All these men assume that women are either perfect or devils; they never think of them as human. Hence they never learn that relationships need careful negotiation and recognition of individuality.
- Only Petruccio brings about a change – whatever we think of his methods, he sees them as applying to an individual, a woman he was 'born to tame'.

**2.** 'Shakespeare's use of food in the play is central to our understanding of some of its key themes.' To what extent do you agree with this statement?

- Yes – the play is structured around two major feasts.
- They symbolise harmony and happiness – their success or failure tells us about relationships.
- Katherina has to learn the value of social rituals, so doesn't get to attend her own feast.
- All is harmony at Bianca's wedding feast – until the two marriages show flaws.

- In Petruccio's house, food is the bedrock of domestic comfort. He wants to show Katherina a house deprived of this by bad temper, and ensures food is wasted and servants upset.
- Food imagery underpins the play's treatment of social relationships. This has to be seen alongside the scenes between the individual couples – their more personal interactions are just as important, as love is private as well as the basis of social harmony.

**3.** How are verse and prose conventions used to express personal and social relationships?

- By common convention Sly speaks quite naturalistic prose – but when he begins to believe he is a Lord he tries verse, so the convention is parodied. Is this also a parody of rigid class relations?
- Their disguises reveal the tutors as quite inept at music and Latin. Again, perhaps a joke about class relations – as tutors they should be fluent.
- Lucentio and Hortensio use courtly love images of conventional beauty – do they see the real Bianca?
- Petruccio uses many kinds of language and this suggests he is at ease with himself. For example, he uses mock-heroic verse to boast to the men but to Katherina he uses fast prose jokes and verse in praise of her dark beauty.
- Katherina uses very formal rhetorical verse for her long speech – but is it also a declaration of love for Petruccio?
- The most attractive characters can play with conventions of verse and language; those who follow them slavishly do not have very satisfactory relationships.

# Part Five: Contexts and Interpretations

## Section One: Check your understanding

**1.** Consider a scene from *The Taming of the Shrew* alongside one from a play from a different period that also explores the nature of marriage.

- At the end of *The Taming Of The Shrew* Katherina has little choice but to stay married. Ibsen's *A Doll's House* (1879) ends with Nora leaving her husband and assuming there may be a divorce.
- Ibsen's heroine can envisage a life in which she could work for wages. This is not an option for Katherina – house and work are the same.
- The focus has shifted decisively – Ibsen's play is about a woman; while Katherina is a key character, the last scene is about Petruccio's triumph.

**2.** What do we know about the economic status of Christopher Sly in Elizabethan society?

- Sly says in the Induction 2.15 that he is a tinker – an itinerant mender of pots and pans.
- Is this a step down in the world? He has also been a cardmaker, vital to the Warwickshire wool industry.
- He can point to a place of residence, so cannot be whipped as a vagrant – he is not at the very bottom of the social ladder.
- He gets credit at the ale-house, so must earn something.

**3.** What does the play tell us about boy players?

- They use a 'soft, low tongue' (Induction 1.113), i.e. they modulate their voices to sound feminine.
- They can be seductive – Sly is very taken with his 'wife'.
- They can be contrasting physical types, like Katherina and Bianca.
- The play holds up standards of 'feminine' submissiveness and beauty – the fact that the female parts are not played by women underlines that the standards are impossible.

**4.** Who would you describe as the most powerful person in the play, and why?

- The Lord in the Induction controls more people and property than anyone else.
- He is never contradicted – contrast Grumio and Petruccio.
- He exercises power over the minds of the socially vulnerable – nobody in the main play attempts to do more than change Katherina's behaviour.

**5.** What setting suits Katherina best?

- In her home she is unwanted and generally reviled by the suitors – and expresses anger.
- In Petruccio's house she is tired and hungry.
- On the road to Padua she seems to find some entertainment in teasing Vincentio and is interested in watching what happens to Bianca and Lucentio.
- This sugggests that she is most at home when not confined.

**6.** What impressions do we get of Italy?

- Lucentio describes Padua as a 'nursery of arts' (I.1.2) and Baptista's world is one of art and culture.
- The *commedia dell'arte* characters of the subplot are Italian in style – romantic, poetic and typical of Italian theatre conventions in that they are not very complex.
- It provides a contrast to the noisy, sport-loving Warwickshire of the opening scene.

**7.** How might an adaptation of the play tell you something about the period that produced it?

- Adaptations from the period following the Second World War – such as *Kiss Me, Kate* – stress the farcical element, but do not alter the play's gender relations.
- This reflects their concern that women should return to the home, not continue working.
- Contemporary adaptations – such as Sally Wainwright's version for *ShakespeaRE-Told* – search for motivation for the characters.
- This shows that the original plot is not wholly acceptable – we need to see why Katherina and Petruccio might find a relationship as individuals, but the story cannot be seen as a recipe for any marriage.

**8.** Compare two differing critical views about the scenes at Petruccio's house in Act IV and consider which best reflects your own understanding.

- Katherina's hunger and her need to plead for food are comic in Aristotle's terms, because temporary.

- Hence, when she thanks Petruccio for the meat she has learnt something about herself – Act IV is a low point, but a chance for personal growth.
- A feminist study might see the same episode as a demonstration of a husband's power – Petruccio is showing her that she is totally dependent on him.
- It might also note Katherina's isolation as the only female figure – the male servants share Petruccio's Elizabethan assumption that women are a 'problem' to be solved.

**9.** The play has been seen as reflecting the marriage debates in Elizabethan England. What questions might it have provoked among its female spectators at the time? Make a brief list.

- Does the 'obedience' you vow to your husband in the marriage service always involve following his orders literally?
- If a woman has given no consent at all, is her marriage binding?
- What sort of say should she have in the choice of a husband?
- Are man and wife like king and subject? If so, what are his responsibilities?
- Do women really talk too much? Can a man talk too much? How much is too much?

**10.** What sort of effect might casting have on the way the play is understood?

- It is a popular play for acknowledged couples – this can soften some of the brutality and focus on the unspoken attraction between Katherina and Petruccio.
- In single-sex productions (all-male or all-female) the audience is more aware of the play as a play, so less involved with the characters, and more aware of gender relations in general.
- Casting a 'star' as Petruccio or Katherina will probably tilt the balance of sympathy accordingly.

### Section Two: Working towards the exam

**1.** '*The Taming of the Shrew* is about power rather than about love.' To what extent do you agree with this statement?

- YES: the Induction frames the play in a story about a powerful man's total dominance over a poor one.
- YES: money rules in Padua, and men control the money.
- YES: Petruccio has all the power in the marriage. Katherina must conform or suffer.
- NO: the Lord is not an admirable character – the players present something more complex than his own game. An implied rebuke?
- NO: *Commedia* conventions depend on the idea that 'love finds a way' and we should support the young lovers over the old men.
- NO: Katherina's marriage is a process of negotiation. She and Petruccio tacitly agree in I.2 that he will not 'cuff' her if she does not hit anybody. Similar negotiations occur in the 'sun and moon' dispute.
- NO: Katherina's final speech is an act of obedience, but it stresses love – though in terms more acceptable to its original audience than today.

**2.** Does *The Taming of the Shrew* offer any positive images of marriage?

- Yes, but not necessarily of marriages. The text imagines possibilities that are not always fulfilled by the couples, but they are there, for example:
  - Marriage as free choice – although Bianca and Lucentio are at odds at the end, we would not want to see her married to Gremio.
  - 'the special thing' (II.1.127) – Baptista at least pays lip service to the idea of love as the motive for marriage.
  - 'peace … and love, and quiet life' (V.2.114) – Petruccio knows what he is aiming for. Although he thinks that 'awful rule and right supremacy' (line 115) is a precondition of it, it is an attractive image of domestic life.
- Of the marriages that we actually see, Katherina and Petruccio offer some positive images – their game with Vincentio, their kiss in the street, both indicate playfulness and attraction.
- For Shakespeare's audience the demand for obedience in marriage would not seem unreasonable.
- If we put the play in its context, Katherina's final speech treats it as a reward for the man's 'painful labour' (V.2.155). This is, at least, an image of partnership, and one that for an Elizabethan audience would carry a positive message.

**3.** Using examples from stage and screen performance to inform your judgement, as well as your own reading, explain how our understanding of *The Taming of the Shrew* can be influenced by the way Katherina's final speech is performed.

- The speech contains a great deal of argument that is not particularly personal – it is a performance, a set piece.
- There is no indication of Katherina's state of mind – this is a decision for the actor, and the manner of delivery will establish it for the audience.
- Shakespeare's audience would have appreciated the rhetorical skill involved – Katherina is taking the stage.
- This might suggest her endorsement of what she is saying – a happy ending in Elizabethan terms.
- Later performers have ironised the speech – Mary Pickford gave her sister a broad wink, suggesting an affectionate indulgence of her husband's need to feel like the boss.
- This will mean that the whole taming process needs to be treated as broad comedy with no painful consequences (Pickford learns that it is a trick early in the film).
- It ignores Katherina's genuinely painful situation within the family.
- Explicitly feminist productions, such as Ed Hall's and Yucel Erten's, have ended with the speech delivered as if Katherina is brainwashed into submission (in Erten's production, it was the prelude to suicide).
- This means we view the whole of the taming process in this way. This is possible – but we may find the subplot jarring.
- There is increasing use of the Induction to provide distance – this allows us to accept that the play is not wholly consistent.

# MARK SCHEME

Use this page to assess your answer to the **Practice task** on page 98.

Look at the elements listed for each Assessment Objective. Examiners will be looking to award the highest grades to the students who meet the majority of these criteria. If you can meet two to three elements from each AO, you are working at a good level, with some room for improvement to a higher level.*

> **'Although the play is a comedy, Shakespeare's presentation of gender relations undermines the laughter.'**
>
> **By considering Shakespeare's dramatic methods, to what extent do you agree with this view?**

| **AO1** | Articulate informed, personal and creative responses to literary texts, using associated concepts and terminology, and coherent, accurate written expression. | <ul><li>You make a range of clear, relevant points about gender relations in the play.</li><li>You use a range of literary terms correctly, e.g. **foreshadowing, metaphor, metatheatre, irony, dialogue**.</li><li>You write a clear introduction, outlining your thesis and provide a clear conclusion.</li><li>You signpost and link your ideas fluently about gender relations within the play.</li><li>You offer an overall personal interpretation or conceptualisation of the text that is well-argued and convincing.</li></ul> |
| --- | --- | --- |
| **AO2** | Analyse ways in which meanings are shaped in literary texts. | <ul><li>You explain the techniques and methods Shakespeare uses to present relationships between men and women.</li><li>You explain in detail how such examples shape meaning, e.g. scenes of courtship (Bianca and the suitors), scenes between husband and wife (Petruccio and Katherina) and scenes between fathers and daughters (e.g. Act I, Scene 1).</li><li>You comment on how the dialogue, such as the 'flyting' in Act I and Katherina's attempts to stop Petruccio bullying the servants in Act IV, represents the way female freedom is curtailed by marriage.</li></ul> |
| **AO3** | Demonstrate understanding of the significance and influence of the contexts in which literary texts are written and received. | <ul><li>You demonstrate your understanding of comic tropes and motifs – for instance, the assumption that a wedding feast will signal a happy ending (and the fact that Shakespeare uses two, neither of which is altogether pleasant).</li><li>Literary context: the use of *commedia dell'arte* stereotypes, especially the older men.</li><li>Historical context: the marriage debates of the period.</li></ul> |
| **AO4** | Explore connections across literary texts. | <ul><li>You make relevant links between characters and ideas, noting how, for example, Katherina's shrewish but witty tongue is repeatedly silenced by her father or treated as a problem by the men, while in *Much Ado About Nothing* Beatrice is an attractive woman desired by more than one man.</li></ul> |
| **AO5** | Explore literary texts informed by different interpretations. | <ul><li>Where appropriate, you incorporate and comment on critics' views of the extent to which all of the marriages at the end can be seen as potentially problematic.</li><li>You assert your own independent view clearly.</li></ul> |

* This mark scheme gives you a broad indication of attainment, but check the specific mark scheme for your paper/task to ensure you know what to focus on.